The New York Times
Great Songs of ABBA

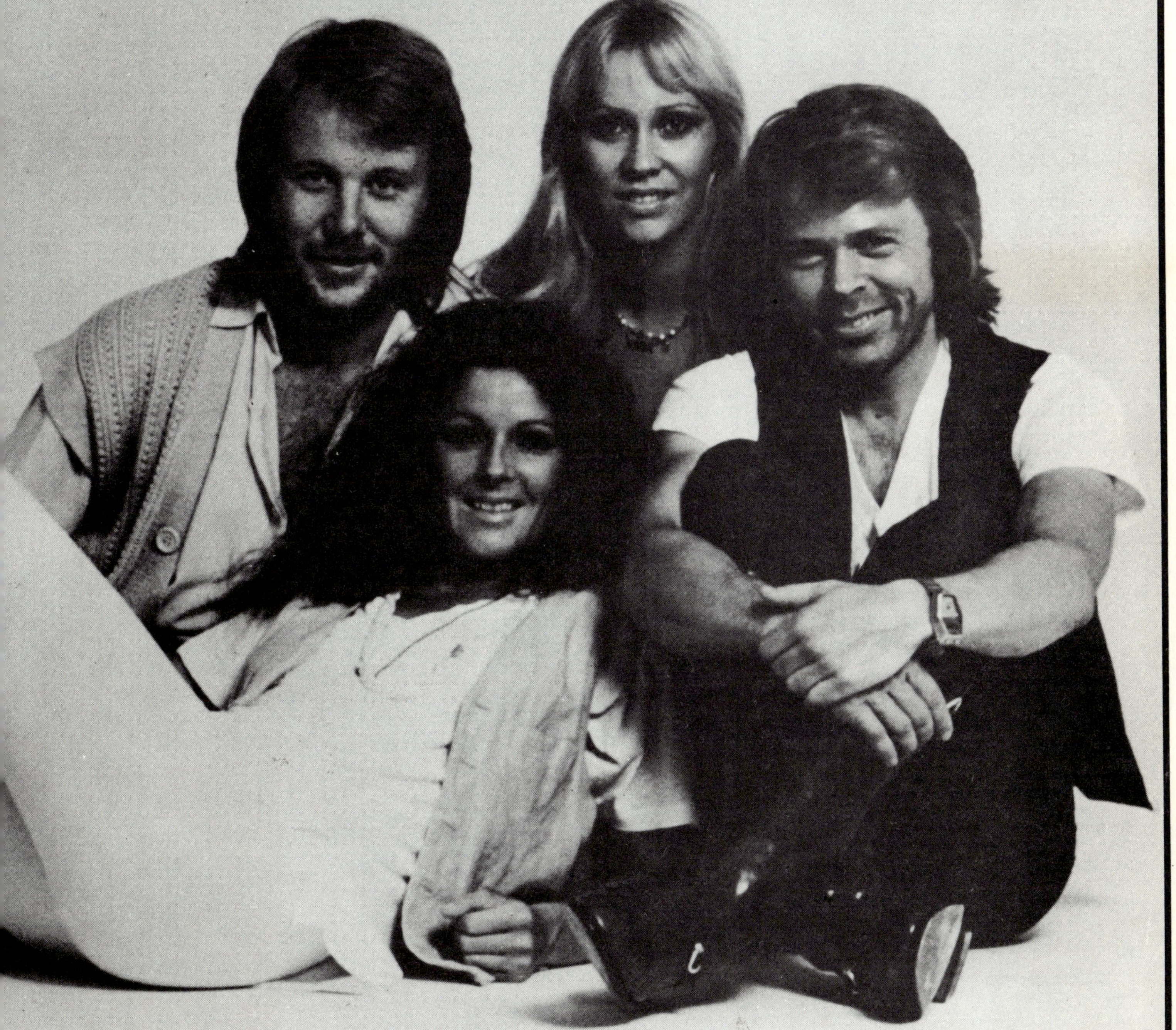

Arranged and Edited by
Milton Okun

Published by CHERRY LANE MUSIC CO., INC.
P.O. Box 4247
Greenwich, CT 06830

© Copyright 1980 CHERRY LANE MUSIC CO., INC.

All rights reserved. No part of this book may be reproduced or transmitted in any form or by any electronic or mechanical means including photocopying, information storage and retrieval systems without permission in writing from the publisher except by a reviewer who may quote brief passages in a review.

As to all musical compositions in this book, international copyright secured; all rights reserved including public performance for profit. Any copying, arranging or adapting of the compositions without the consent of the copyright owner is an infringement of copyright.

Library of Congress Catalog Card Number: 79-54690
International Standard Book Number: 0-8129-0896-1

Manufactured in the United States of America

Arranged and Edited by Milton Okun

Associate Music Editor - Dan Fox

Art Director - Gil Gjersvik

Music Engraving - Armando Dal Molin, Music Typographers

Photographs courtesy of Hanser/Polar Music Int'l AB and Ivan Mogull Music Corporation

Sole Selling Agent for Countless Songs, Ltd. and Artwork Music Co., Inc.: Ivan Mogull Music Corporation, New York, New York

These arrangements Copyright © 1980 by Artwork Music Co., Inc. and Countless Songs, Ltd., where applicable.

The publisher wishes to express its sincere gratitude to Mr. Ivan Mogull for his invaluable assistance and advice.

ABBA

Page	Title
6	Introduction
8	Biography
10	Performance Notes
12	Angeleyes
17	Another Town, Another Train
20	Arrival
22	As Good As New
30	Bang-A-Boomerang
40	Chiquitita
46	Dance (While The Music Still Goes On)
52	Dancing Queen
58	Does Your Mother Know
67	Dum Dum Diddle
35	Eagle
62	Fernando
72	Gonna Sing You My Lovesong
78	Hasta Mañana
82	He Is Your Brother
86	Hey, Hey Helen
90	Hole In Your Soul
96	Honey, Honey
105	I Do, I Do, I Do, I Do, I Do
100	I Have A Dream
109	I Wonder (Departure)
116	If It Wasn't For The Nights
112	I'm A Marionette
123	Intermezzo No. 1
130	I've Been Waiting For You
145	The King Has Lost His Crown
159	King Kong Song

134 Kisses Of Fire
150 Knowing Me, Knowing You
166 Lovers (Live A Little Longer)
140 Mamma Mia
172 Man In The Middle
176 Money, Money, Money
191 Move On
182 My Love, My Life
213 My Mama Said
201 The Name Of The Game
221 Nina, Pretty Ballerina
154 One Man, One Woman
224 People Need Love
230 Ring, Ring
234 Rock Me
186 Sitting In The Palmtree
238 So Long
242 SOS
246 Suzy-Hang-Around
250 Take A Chance On Me
196 Thank You For The Music
208 That's Me
256 Tiger
260 Tropical Loveland
216 Voulez-Vous
264 Watch Out
270 Waterloo
267 What About Livingstone
274 When I Kissed The Teacher
279 Why Did It Have To Be Me?

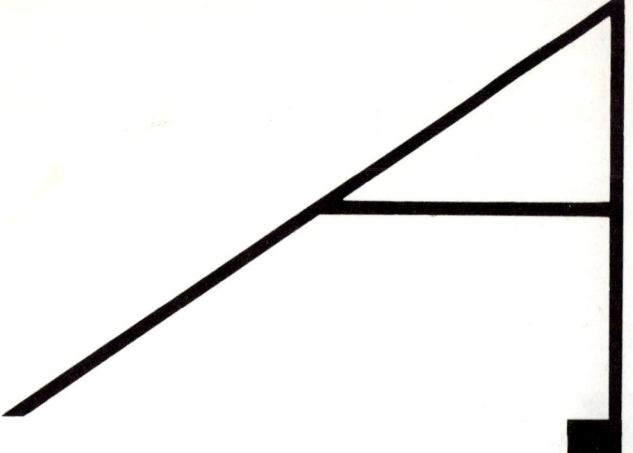

To enter the domain of popular music is to embark on a journey down an ever-changing and constantly moving path. In this world are hundreds and thousands of singers and songwriters, groups and individuals alike, with something to say in song. They come and go. Once in a while one or two may break through, and with a lot of luck, a single release can hit the charts. An album follows, then an exhausting schedule of one-night concerts, and T.V. and radio appearances. And so it goes. On the top one minute and perhaps falling into oblivion the next. A few years later the song is nothing more than a relationship between time and place; a short and meaningless trip down memory lane. And that is all.

But for some, it's different. For some, the music lingers...and what was good gets better. It is influenced (but not bound) by time and place, or culture or the state of the economy. The music makes you feel good, or, perhaps, it makes you think, but it affects you somehow, in some way, for a very long time.

There are very few in the history of popular music that have made such an impact. Elvis Presley, Nat King Cole, Frank Sinatra and the Beatles come to mind.

...and ABBA. Since 1974 when they took Australia and Europe by storm with their explosive hit *Waterloo* (at the Eurovision Song Contest), ABBA's success has been marked by an awesome track record of hits. In Europe, Australia, Asia, Japan, the Middle East, and parts in between, they compare the ABBA phenomenon with the Beatles' domination of the sixties.

ABBA. The neat and handy abbreviation for Agnetha, Björn, Benny and Anni-Frid; Sweden's most successful export since "smorgasbord" and Volvo cars.

But, in the beginning, there was no ABBA. No plans for world-wide stardom. And maybe, most conspicuously, no girls. In the beginning there were only Björn and Benny. Each pursuing separate careers and writing good, popular songs. Both seemed destined to lead comfortable lives composing, performing and producing. They met for the first time in 1966 and the musical "chemistry" between composer and pianist clicked. Two short years later they joined forces and by 1970 Agnetha and Anni-Frid completed the quartet for their first gig in Gothenburg, Sweden.

In the early seventies, ABBA didn't perform together as they do today. The girls waited on the sidelines while Benny and Björn pursued their prime interests in composing and producing. They walked off with first prize for Best Lyrics at the Tokyo Song Festival 1972, in collaboration with their manager and mentor Stig Anderson. Shortly after that, the foursome got together on a record release entitled *People Need Love*.

Today, seven years and seven albums later, the ABBA sounds of swirling textures, intricate rhythms, and soaring melodies have attracted millions of record buyers throughout the world. Both Björn and Benny, the musical "engineers" behind all the statistics, are

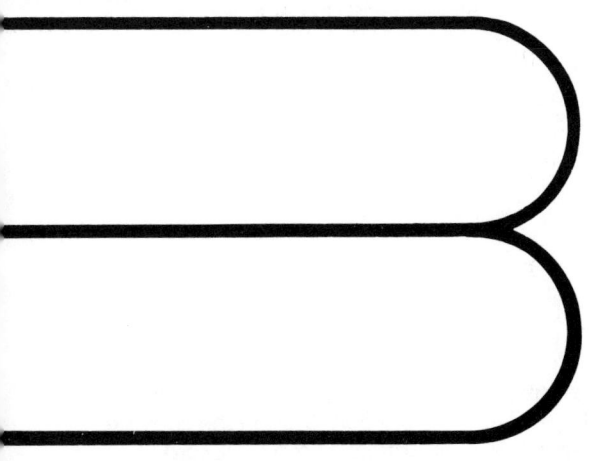

convinced that their staying power and record-breaking world appeal has more than a little to do with the fact that ABBA's music closes the generation gap. "We write tuneful melodies that seem to appeal to both the young and the old," they assert. "That's especially noticeable in Australia. There, we've played concerts to huge 35,000 plus audiences where we've literally had both the nine and the ninety year olds. Only the punk crowd seems to stay away completely from our music..."

Maybe so. But punks and new wave rockers may very well have sneaked a glimpse when ABBA were featured guests on prime time U.S. television with Olivia Newton-John. Or, in January of 1979 when ABBA presented their song *Chiquitita* on UNICEF's charity gala from the United Nations Building in New York surrounded by the Bee Gees, Donna Summer, and other star chart busters.

Like the Beatles before them, ABBA adapt and mold many current styles to their own. Although most of their songs can be called mainstream pop-rock, many have other more exotic influences. For example, *Arrival* and *Intermezzo No. 1* are both almost Baroque in quality; *I Have A Dream* and *I Wonder* are slow, pretty ballads; a bitter-sweet almost Brechtian feeling permeates *Money, Money, Money* and *I'm A Marionette*; *Sitting In The Palmtree* and *Tropical Loveland* show a reggae influence; *Why Did It Have To Be Me?* is boogie; *Lovers*, *Angeleyes*, *If It Wasn't For The Nights*, and *Voulez-Vous* are disco. Also represented are gospel (*People Need Love*), waltz (*Move On*), Mariachi (Mexican street band) music (*Fernando*), and American show tunes (*Thank You For The Music*).

ABBA's originality stems from the distinctive treatment they give to the music of the day. With their usual back-up musicians, Lasse Wellander on guitar, Rutger Gunnarsson playing bass, and Ola Brunkert on drums, ABBA has undeniably achieved the pinnacle of success in Europe. They have been recognized as "Hitmakers of the Year" every year in England since 1974, and have attained the title of "most bootlegged and pirated group in Hong Kong, Taiwan, Singapore and points west." Many of their innumerable hits have made their way high on the U.S. charts: *Ring, Ring*, *Mamma Mia*, *Honey, Honey*, *Rock Me*, *Dancing Queen*, *Money, Money, Money*, and most recently *Chiquitita* and *Does Your Mother Know* from their album *Voulez-vous*.

Managed by Sweden's Number 1 music publisher, Stig Anderson, the success of ABBA is a combination of careful planning, wide appeal and an uncanny facility for writing music that is both lyrically and melodically potent. Their initial success outside their homeland with *Waterloo* was no novelty, but a firm foundation on which they have continued to build year after year. With more hit records to their credit than most groups can hope to accumulate in an entire career, ABBA will most certainly have a tremendous impact on musical trends in the eighties.

AGNETHA

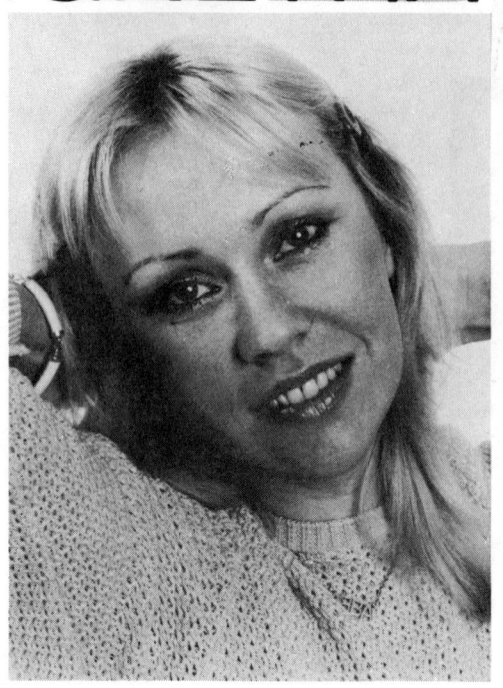

Temperamental, self-assured and ethereal looking, Agnetha Fältskog is the youngest member of ABBA. Though she may be the youngest, Agnetha was a household name for record buyers long before ABBA was formed. She began composing songs at the early age of eight and at fifteen began singing professionally, gaining experience with hometown dance bands. Rumors of Agnetha's talents spread to Germany where she spent a lot of time in television studios at the end of the sixties. By then, she had met Björn, singing back-up vocals and fulfilling nightclub engagements with him.

At one time, Agnetha had a hit album in Sweden, but since joining ABBA, she has cut down on her own writing to concentrate on her singing. Also, Agnetha wrote most of her tunes in her native language, which is, for obvious reasons, not suited for the international market.

Regarding ABBA's success, Agnetha asserts, "...you must develop your talents. No artist is so super important, so super talented that he or she can just sit back and relax. And God knows we in ABBA have worked..."

BENNY

If you believe in pigeon-holing people and filing them under neat catchphrases, then Benny is the cool, laid-back one of ABBA. For Göran Bror "Benny" Andersson, music was always serious business. He grew up lugging an oversized accordion around while learning by trial and error to accompany his father and grandfather, both enthusiastic "squeeze-box" players. Today, he is an accomplished musician on a variety of keyboard instruments.

By the mid-sixties, Benny was part of the Hep Stars, an exuberant Scandinavian band that thrived for some time. When the group faded, they had some fifteen hits to their credit, most of them penned by Benny. He continued on a freelance basis until his meeting with Björn in 1966. Since then, the two have formed a solid, successful partnership responsible for many international hits. Benny credits such artists as the The Eagles, Elton John, and Paul McCartney for his inspiration.

When meeting fans and followers, Benny insists on putting forth his "best efforts." To Benny, "the best" means the up-front singing of Anni-Frid and Agnetha. He tends to understate his own composing contributions and says the girls are THE main reason for the special ABBA sound. You may catch Benny doing some background harmony, but as he himself professes, "...you'll never catch me singing solo. That really sounds terrible..."

ABBA BJÖRN

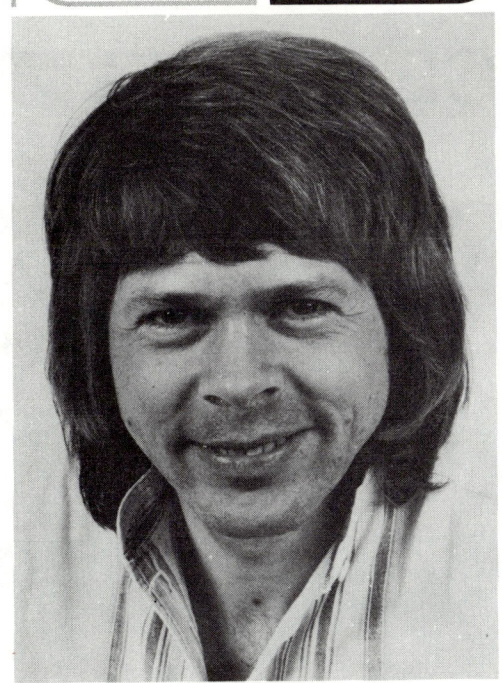

Known as the "Perfectionist" of the ABBA quartet, Björn Christian Ulvaeus expects perfection not only in his career but in his physical appearance as well. In the past six years, Björn has become a full-fledged jogging buff, running some five or six miles a day in suburban Stockholm. With ABBA, he is the one with the patience to get things done.

Like Benny, Björn met pop rock success fairly early. Born in a small town on the Baltic coast of Sweden, Björn formed a group called the West Bay Singers with a few school chums. They were later brought to Stockholm by future ABBA manager Stig Anderson and billed as The Hootenanny Singers.

During this period, Björn wrote original material as well as covering such sizeable hits as Bobby Goldsboro's *Honey* and Jeannie C. Riley's *Harper Valley P.T.A*. But despite his talents in the musical field, Björn had serious doubts about making it a career. He took classes in corporate law which later proved advantageous in ABBA's business ventures.

Björn alleges that all the music he has ever admired has had American roots or origins. To become successful in the U.S., according to Bjorn would be "...the fulfillment of my biggest professional ambition."

ABBA ANNI-FRID

She's tall, slim, and most decidedly, a smart dresser. That's Frida, or Anni-Frid Lyngstad, as cited in her Swedish passport — Norway's gift to Sweden. Frida hails originally from Narvik, an iron export town well above the Midnight Sun latitudes of Norway but came to Stockholm as a little girl. Ever since she can remember, Frida's most fervent ambition was to sing. Of the four ABBA members, she may very well be the one with the broadest knowledge of popular music. She made her vocal debut at the age of ten when she appeared in a local amateur contest. While in her teens, Frida supported herself by fronting a dance band of her own. She went to work in cabaret and television, occasionally touring, and participated in various international song contests.

Frida feels that the vocal aspect alone is not enough for a successful stage performance. Complete choreography of the group is essential for a commanding stage presence. For this reason, Frida keeps herself in shape with daily ballet lessons, convinced that the ABBA stage show benefits from it.

In addition to her success with ABBA, Frida can add motion pictures to her list of personal accomplishments since landing a part in a Swedish movie production. When asked why her pursuits range beyond the musical border, Frida explains, "Any singer/artist has to reload her creative batteries now and then."

ABBA PERFORMANCE NOTES

The arrangements in this collection of ABBA's recorded songs are all in the original recorded keys. This makes it possible for aspiring singers and instrumentalists to play along with the record and learn the subtleties of an authentic sounding performance.

Singers can find the melody easily, as it is always the highest note in the right hand of the piano unless otherwise marked (See example below from *Waterloo*, pg. 270*).

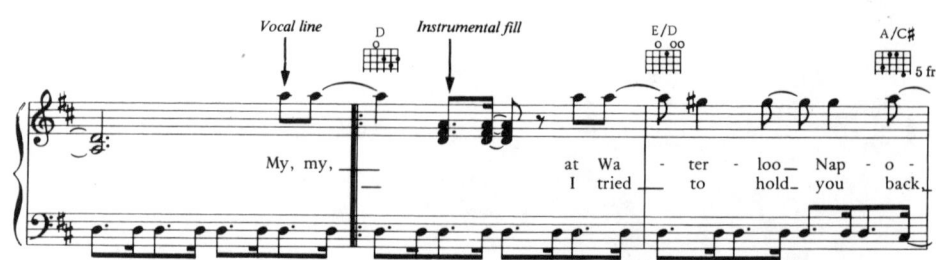

*Copyright © 1974 Union Songs AB, Stockholm, Sweden for the world
Countless Songs Ltd. for U.S.A. and Canada
International Copyright Secured   All Rights Reserved

Since the girls in ABBA sing fairly straight (that is, the notes as written), you will get a good sound by keeping close to what's printed.

Keyboard players (the arrangements can be played on piano, organ, or synthesizer) will find the arrangements satisfying to play. The melody is always in the right hand unless otherwise stated, but in addition, vocal harmonies, guitar licks and other embellishments are included where practical.

In cases where the piano is in a difficult key, appropriate capo directions for guitar are included (See example below from *When I Kissed The Teacher*, pg. 274*).

*Copyright © 1976 Union Songs AB, Stockholm, Sweden for the world
Countless Songs Ltd. for U.S.A. and Canada
International Copyright Secured   All Rights Reserved

Of course, if you're not playing along with the record, or if you're accompanying the voice with guitar alone, you can ignore the capo directions. As a matter of fact, this gives a valuable added flexibility to your vocal range. For example, *Rock Me* (Example below, pg. 234*), is recorded and arranged in the somewhat esoteric key of B major. You can avoid the difficulty of this key for guitar by playing in the key of G with a capo up four frets. But, if the key is a little too high for your vocal range, capo up one or two frets instead. Or, omit the capo entirely. On the other hand, if the vocal range is too low, you can capo up a few more frets than indicated.

*Copyright © 1976 Union Songs AB, Stockholm, Sweden for the world
Countless Songs Ltd. for U.S.A. and Canada
International Copyright Secured   All Rights Reserved

We feel this book will be invaluable to ABBA fans. Not only is it the first comprehensive collection of their recorded songs, but the arrangements are designed to produce a full, professional sound even when performed by one singer accompanied by keyboard and/or guitar. The arrangements also can be adapted for groups by adding bass (from the chord symbols) and drums.

Enjoy!

Angeleyes

Words and Music by
Benny Andersson & Björn Ulvaeus

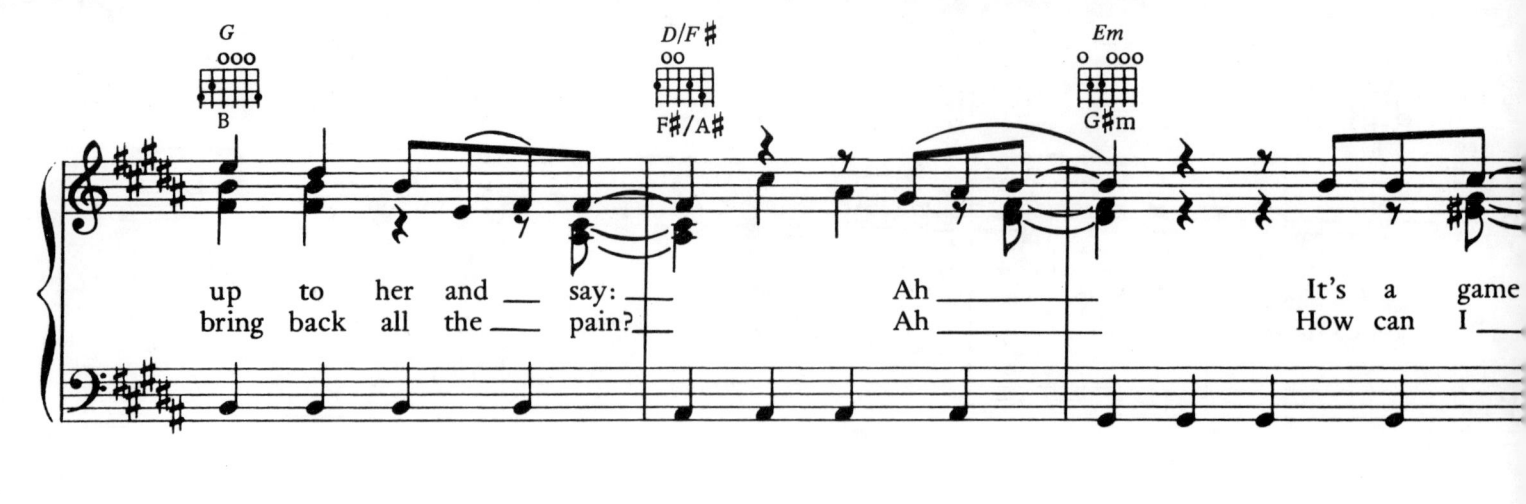
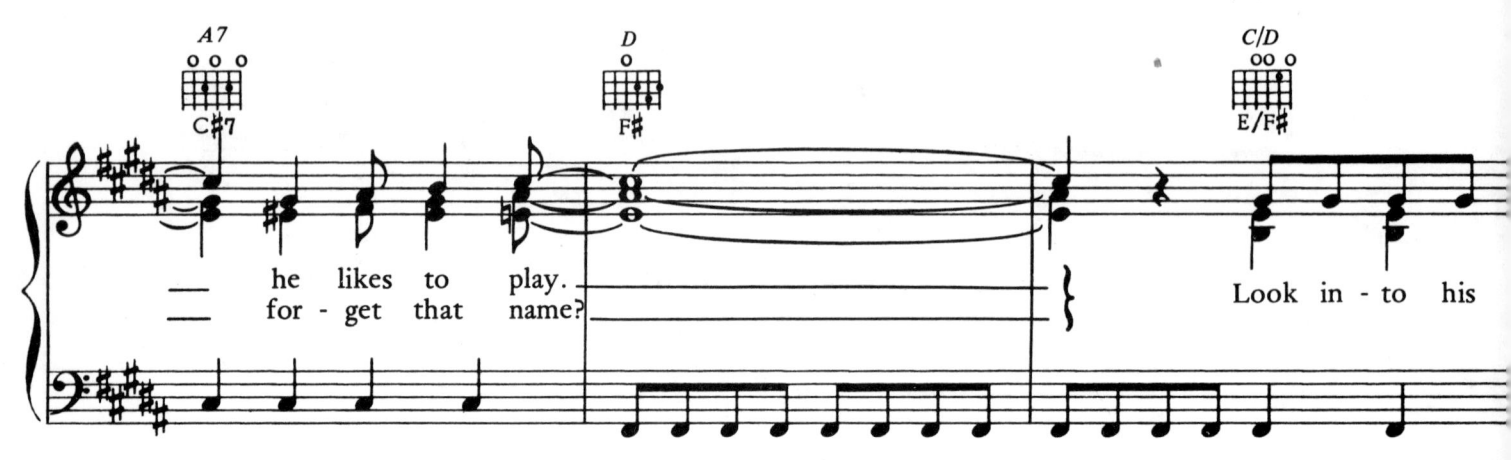

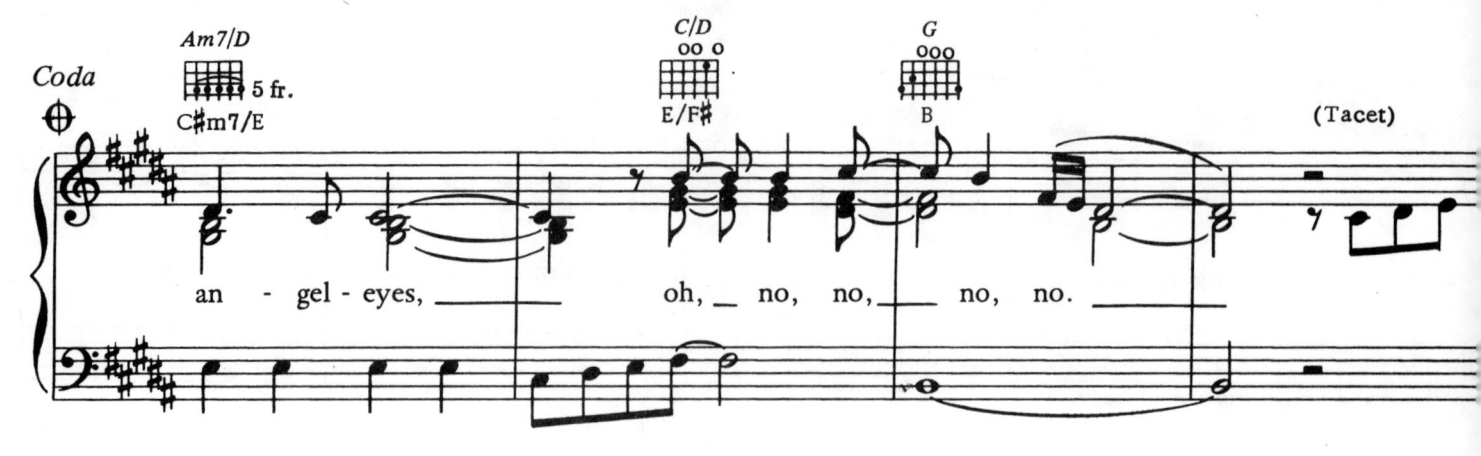

Another Town, Another Train

Words and Music by
Benny Andersson & Björn Ulvaeus

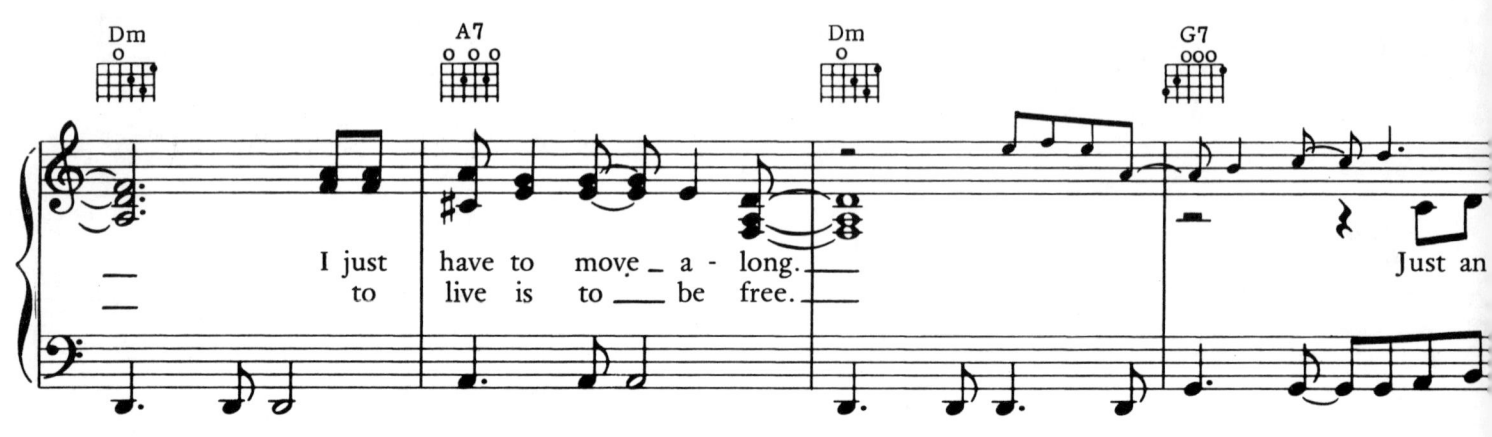

Arrival

Music by
Benny Andersson & Björn Ulvaeus

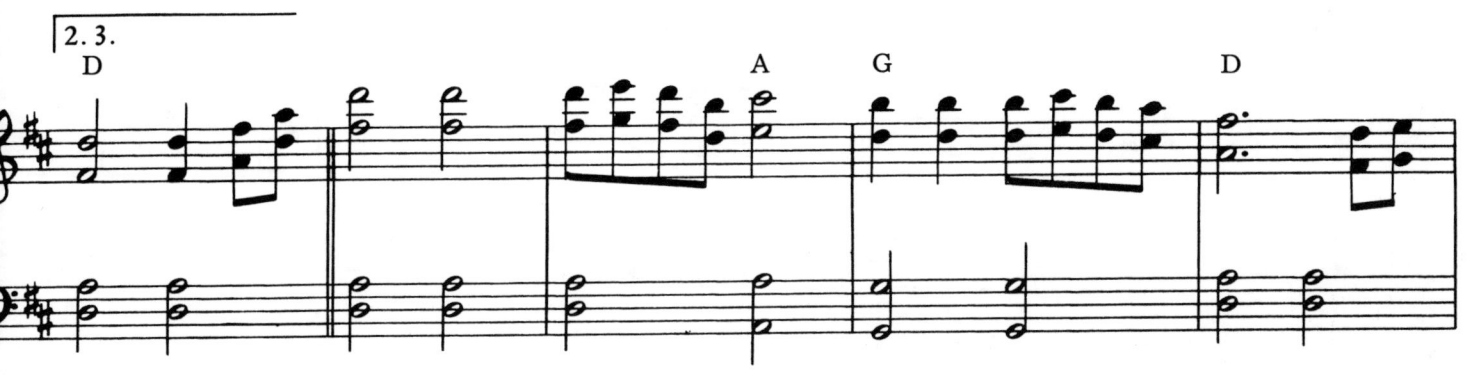

As Good As New

Words and Music by
Benny Andersson & Björn Ulvaeus

* Recorded ½ step lower, in E

Copyright © 1979 Union Songs AB, Stockholm, Sweden for the world
Countless Songs Ltd. for U.S.A. and Canada
International Copyright Secured   All Rights Reserved

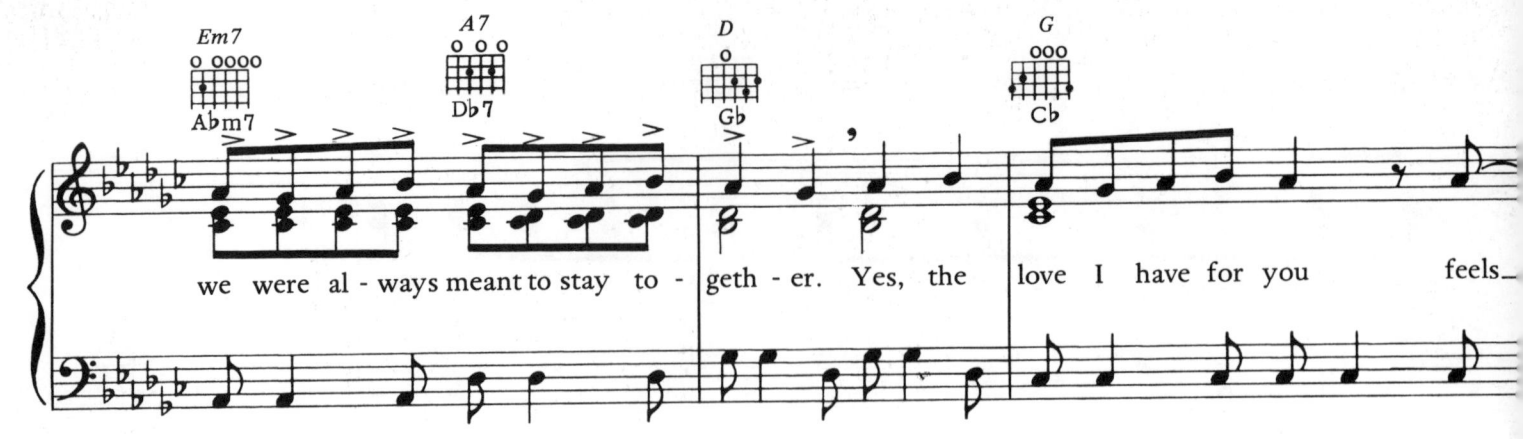

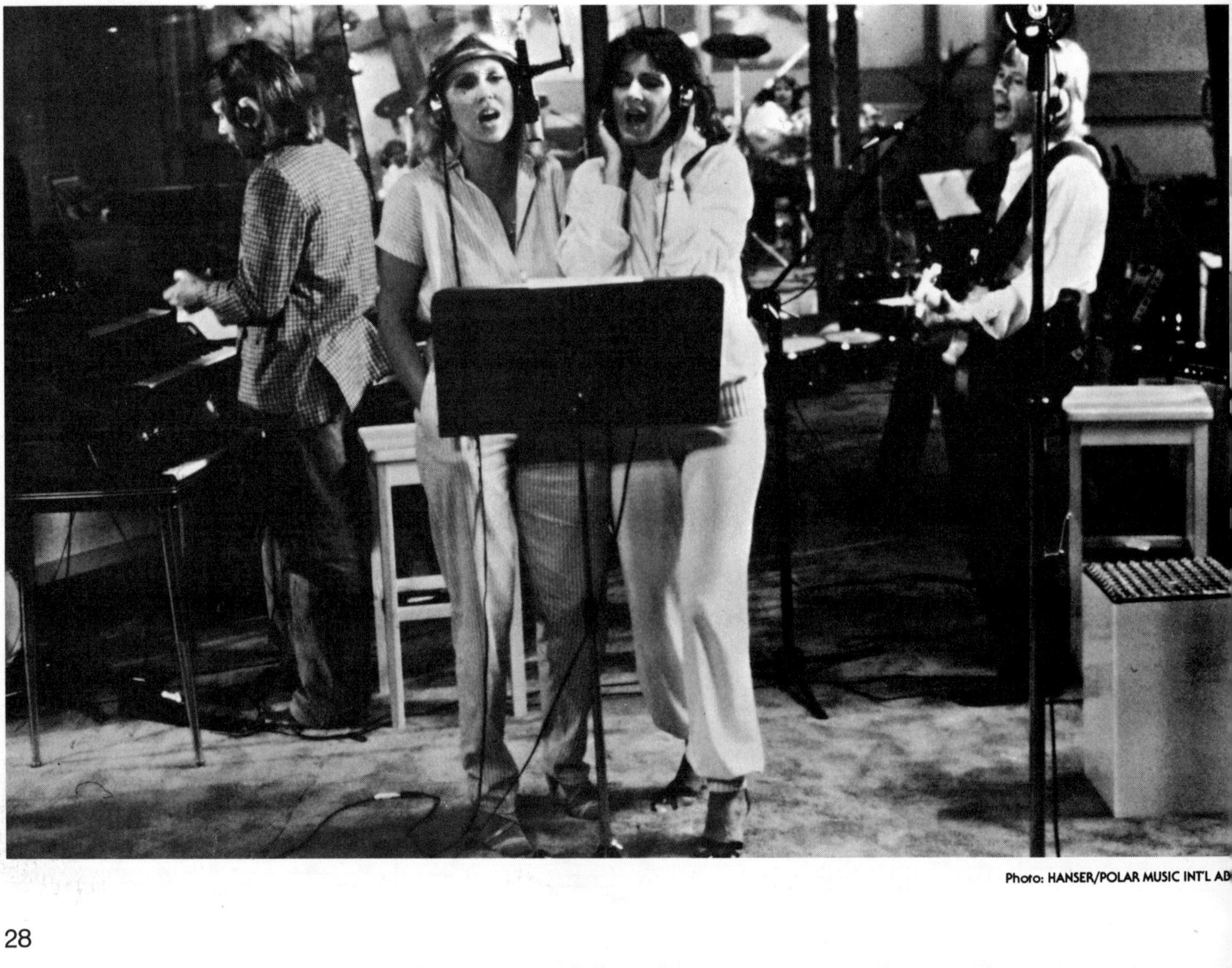

Em7 A7 D G
Abm7 Db7 Gb Cb
we were al - ways meant to stay to - geth - er. Yes, the love I have for you feels

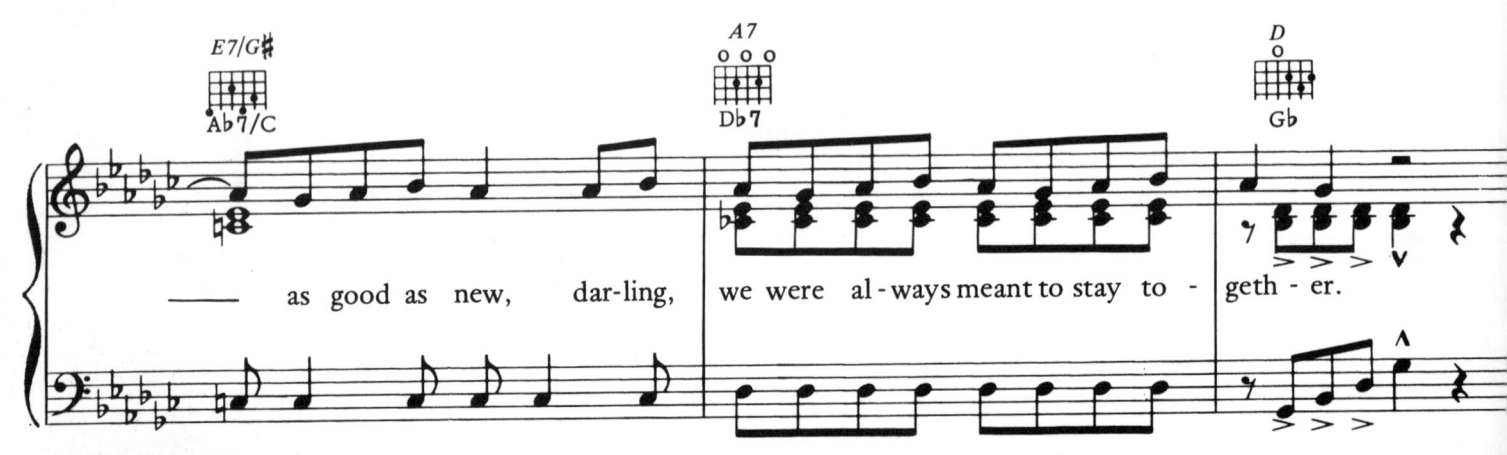

E7/G# A7 D
Ab7/C Db7 Gb
as good as new, dar-ling, we were al - ways meant to stay to - geth - er.

Photo: HANSER/POLAR MUSIC INT'L AB

Gm
3 fr.
C7
F
C7
-mi, dum dum-mi dum - mi dum dum. A bang - a-boom
Gm
3 fr.
C7
-e-boom-e-rang, Love is a tune you hum - my hum hum. By
F
F/Eb
Bb/D
G7
giv-in' a-way I think you'll learn You'll get love in re-turn.
F
C7
To Coda
So bang - a-boom - e-boom-e-rang is love,

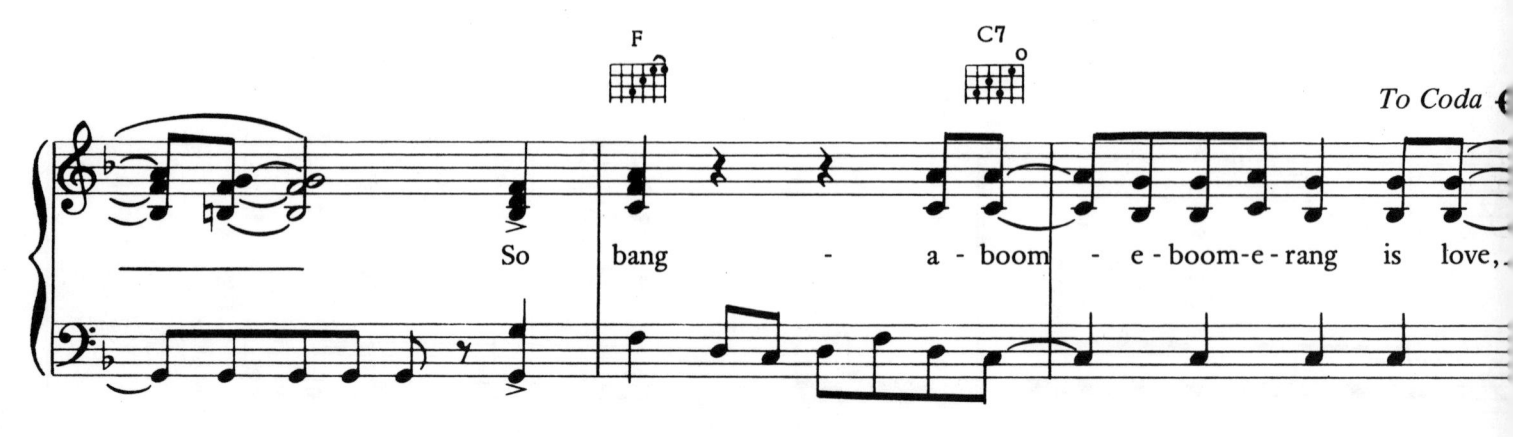

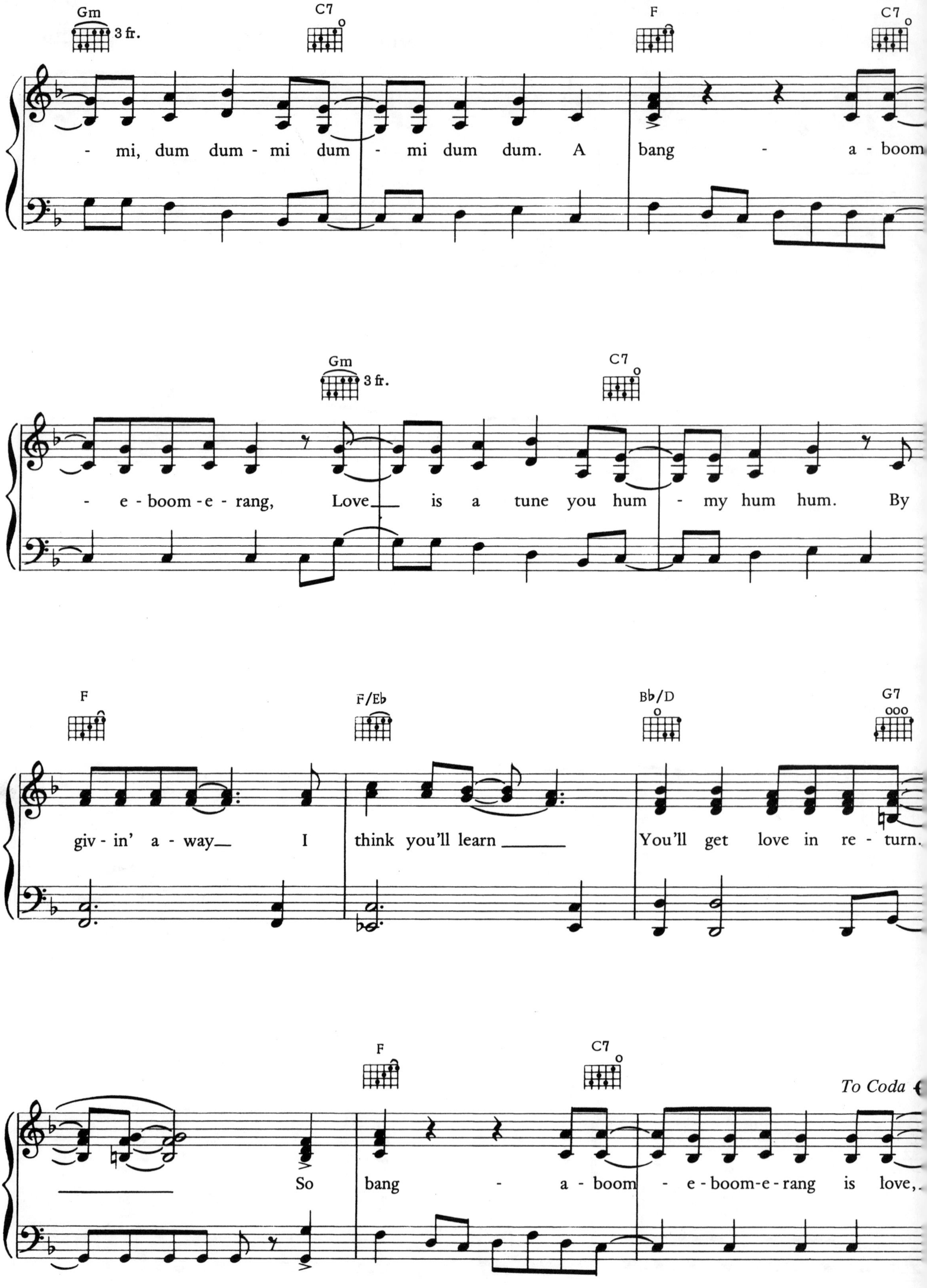

Eagle

Words and Music by
Benny Andersson & Björn Ulvaeus

They came fly-in' from far a-way,___ now I'm un-der their
As all good friends we talk all night___ and we fly wing to

spell.   I love hear-ing the sto-ries that they___
wing,   I have ques-tions and they know ev-'ry-

Copyright © 1977, 1978 Union Songs AB, Stockholm, Sweden for the world
Artwork Music Co., Inc. for U.S.A. and Canada
International Copyright Secured   All Rights Reserved

Chiquitita

Words and Music by
Benny Andersson & Björn Ulvaeus

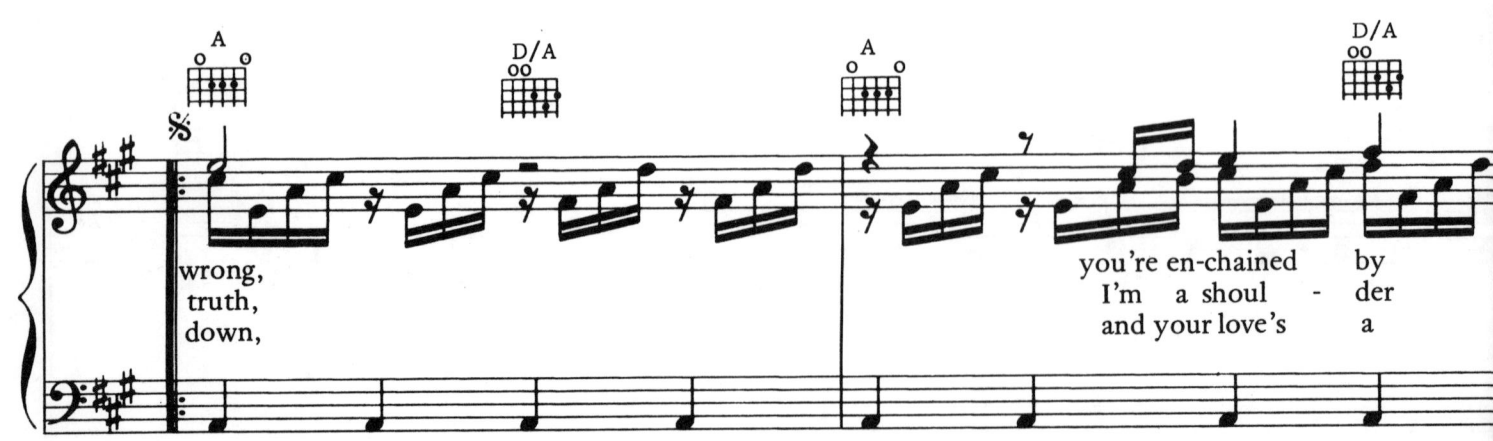

Copyright © 1979 by the Swedish UNICEF-Committee
c/o STIM, P.O. Box 1539, S-111 85 Stockholm
Published in the U.S.A. through UNICEF MUSIC (ASCAP)
Administered by CHAPPELL & CO.,INC.
International Copyright Secured   Used by Permission   All Rights Reserved

Repeat and fade

Dance (While The Music Still Goes On)

Words and Music by
Benny Andersson & Björn Ulvaeus

Copyright © 1973 Union Songs AB, Stockholm, Sweden for the world
Countless Songs Ltd. for U.S.A. and Canada
International Copyright Secured   All Rights Reserved

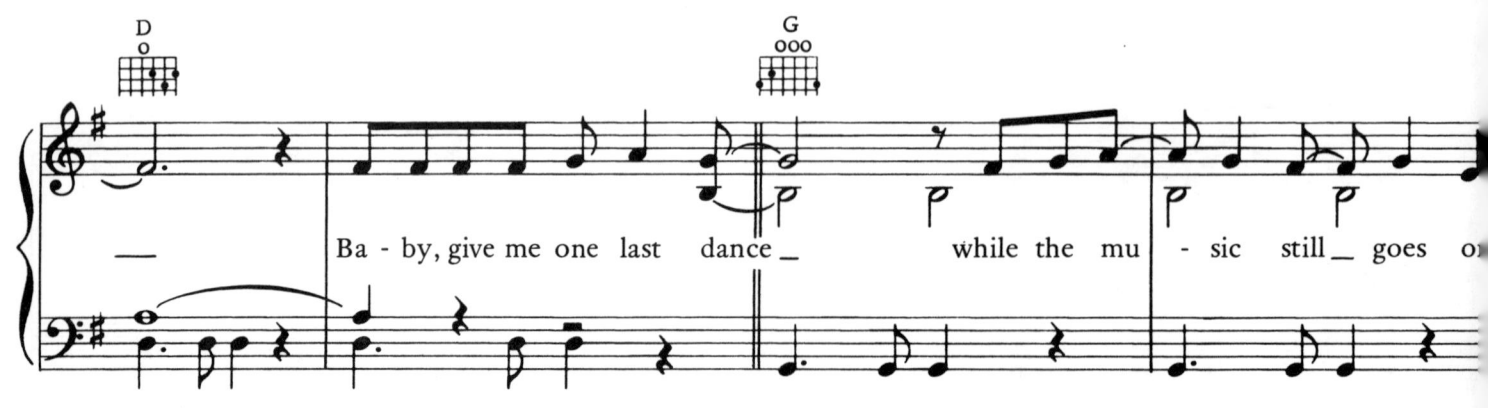

Dancing Queen

Words and Music by
Benny Andersson, Björn Ulvaeus
and Stig Anderson

You can dance, you can jive having the time of your

life. Oh see that girl, watch that scene, dig in the

Copyright © 1976, Polar Music AB, Stockholm, Sweden for the world
Countless Songs Ltd. for U.S.A. and Canada
International Copyright Secured   All Rights Reserved

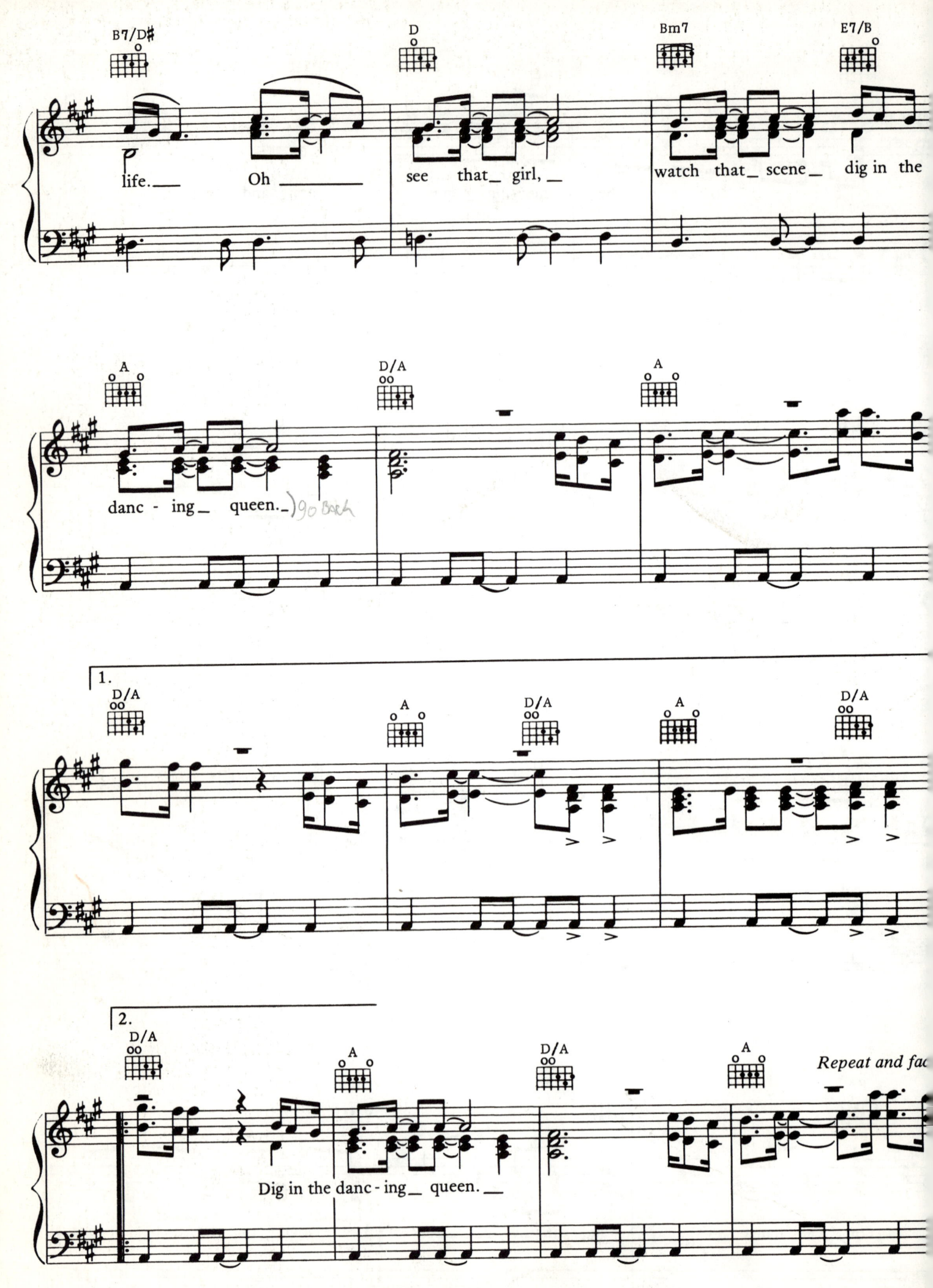

Fernando

*Words and Music by
Benny Andersson, Björn Ulvaeus
and Stig Anderson*

Can you hear the drums, Fer-nan-do?   I re-mem-ber long a-
They were clos-er now, Fer-nan-do.   Ev-'ry hour, ev-'ry min-
Now we're old and grey, Fer-nan-do,   and since man-y years I

go an-oth-er star-ry night like this.   In the fire-light, Fer
ute seemed to last e-ter-nal-ly.   I was so a-fraid Fer
have-n't seen a ri-fle in your hand.   Can you hear the drums, Fer

Copyright © 1975 Union Songs AB, Stockholm, Sweden for the world
Artwork Music Co., Inc. for U.S.A. and Canada
International Copyright Secured   All Rights Reserved

Dum Dum Diddle

Words and Music by
Benny Andersson & Björn Ulvaeus

Coda
G
3 fr.
B
C
E
Em
G♯m
Wish I was dum dum did - dle, your dar -
Repeat and fac
F
A
G
3 fr.
B
C/G
E/B
F/C
A/E
C
E
F/C
A/E
C
E
- ling fid - dle.

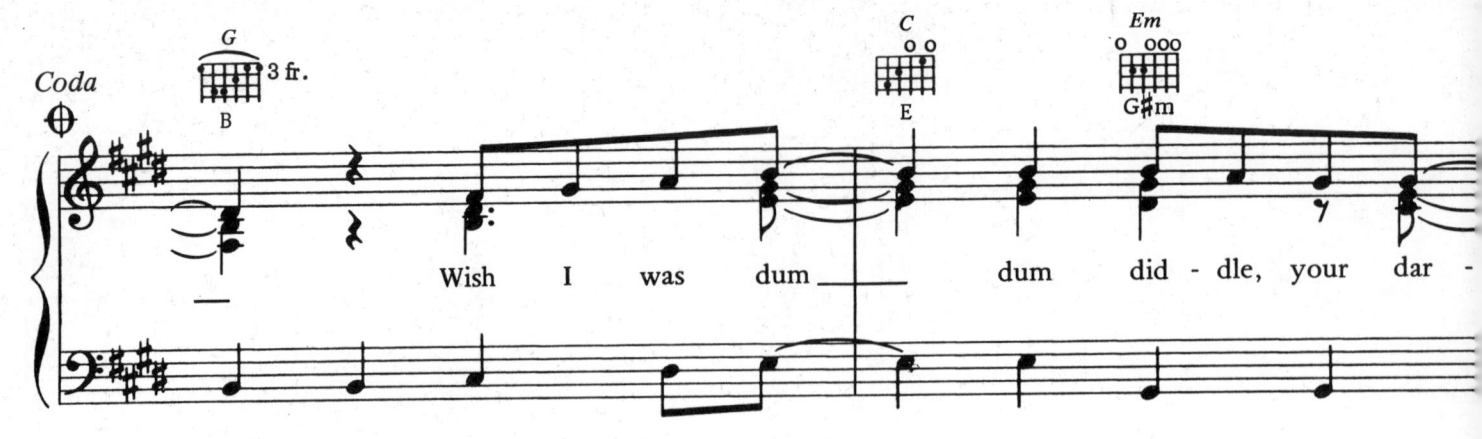

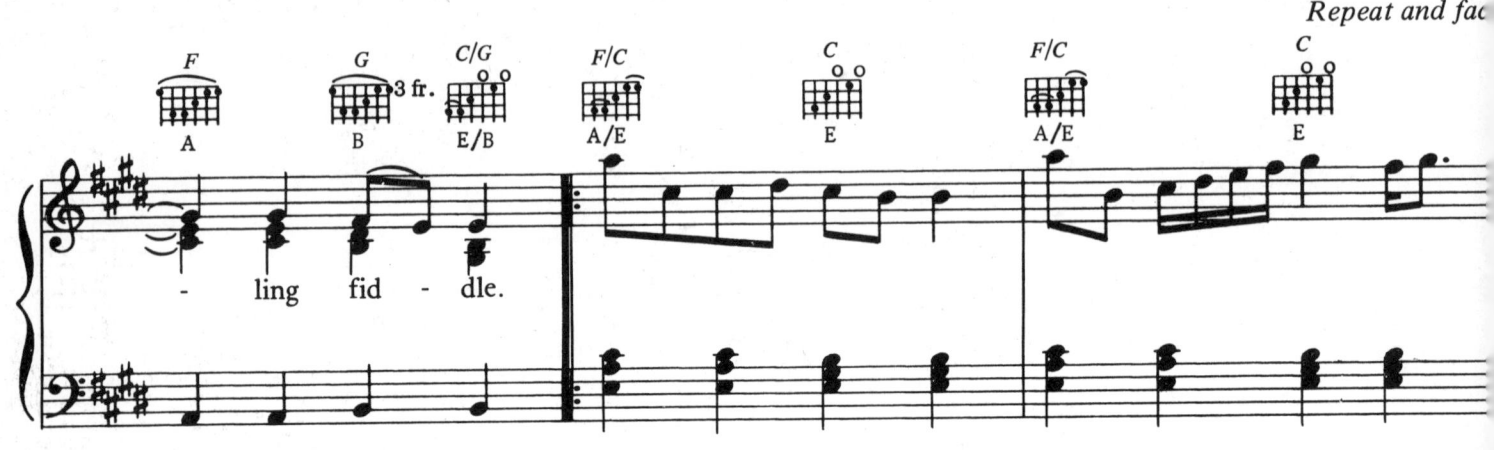

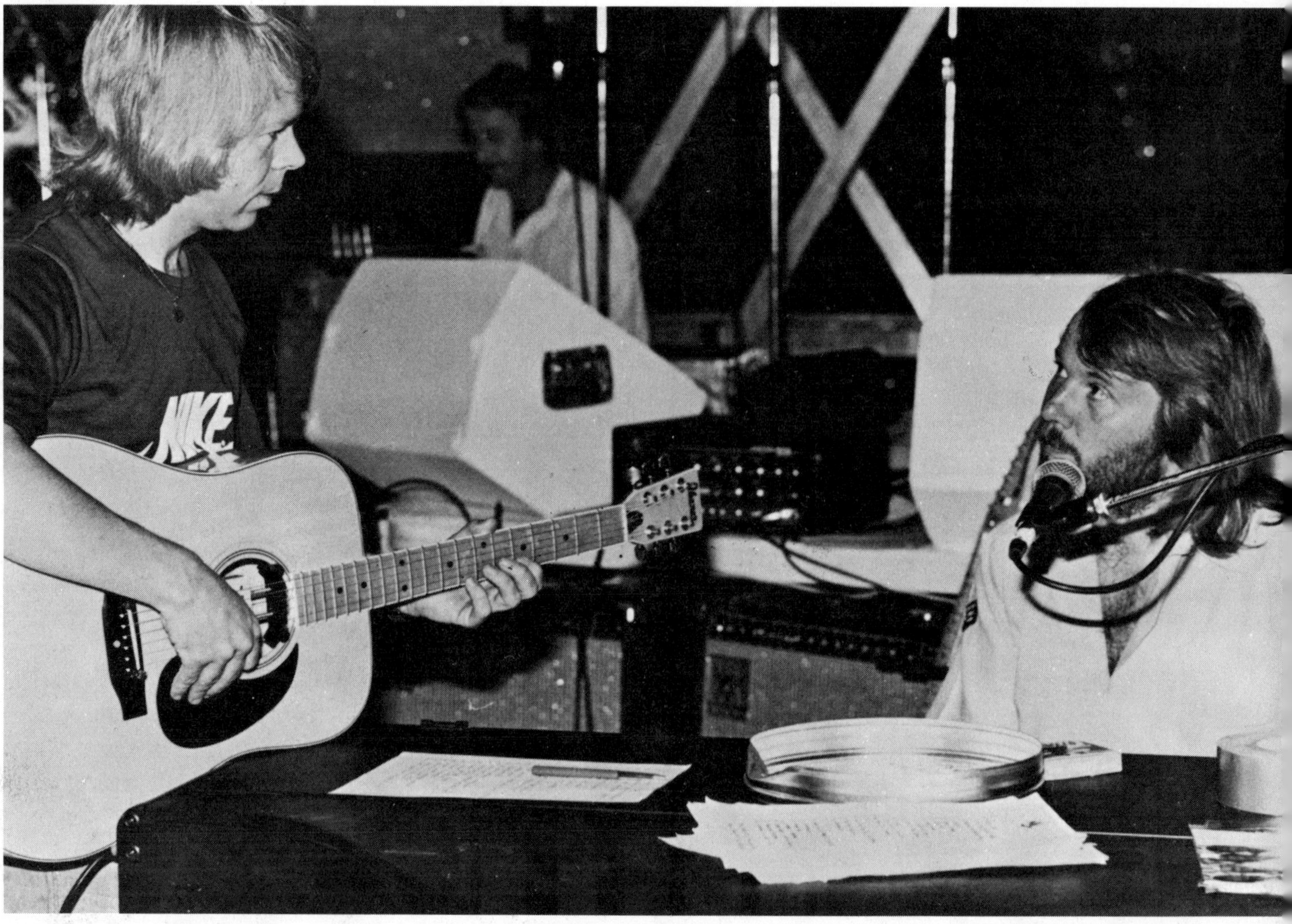

Gonna Sing You My Lovesong

Words and Music by
Benny Andersson & Björn Ulvaeus

Copyright © 1974 Union Songs AB, Stockholm, Sweden for the world
Countless Songs Ltd. for U.S.A. and Canada
International Copyright Secured   All Rights Reserved

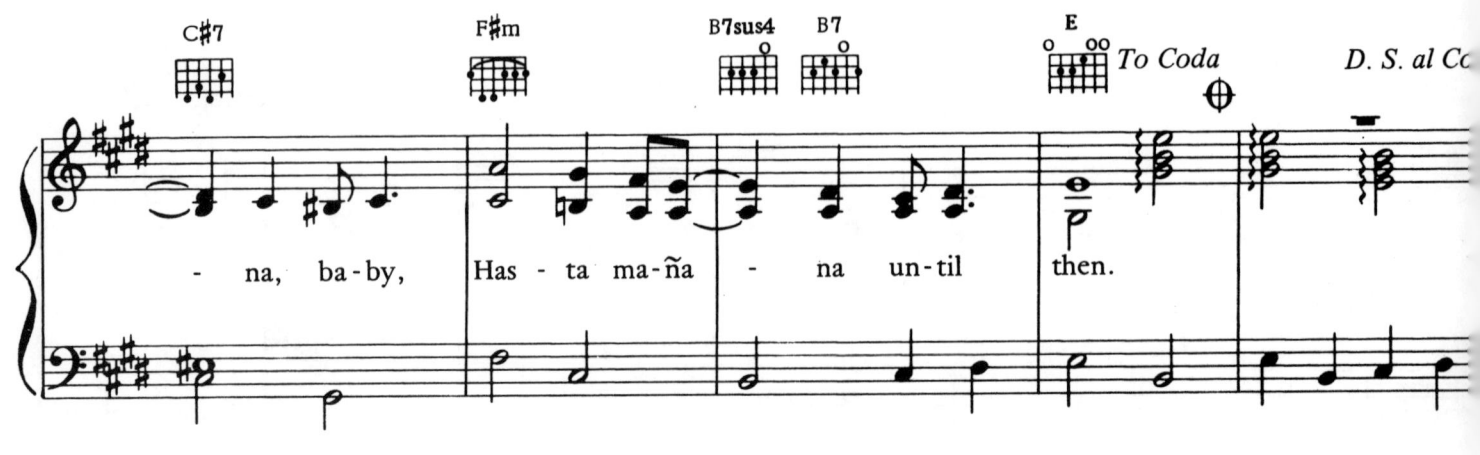

He Is Your Brother

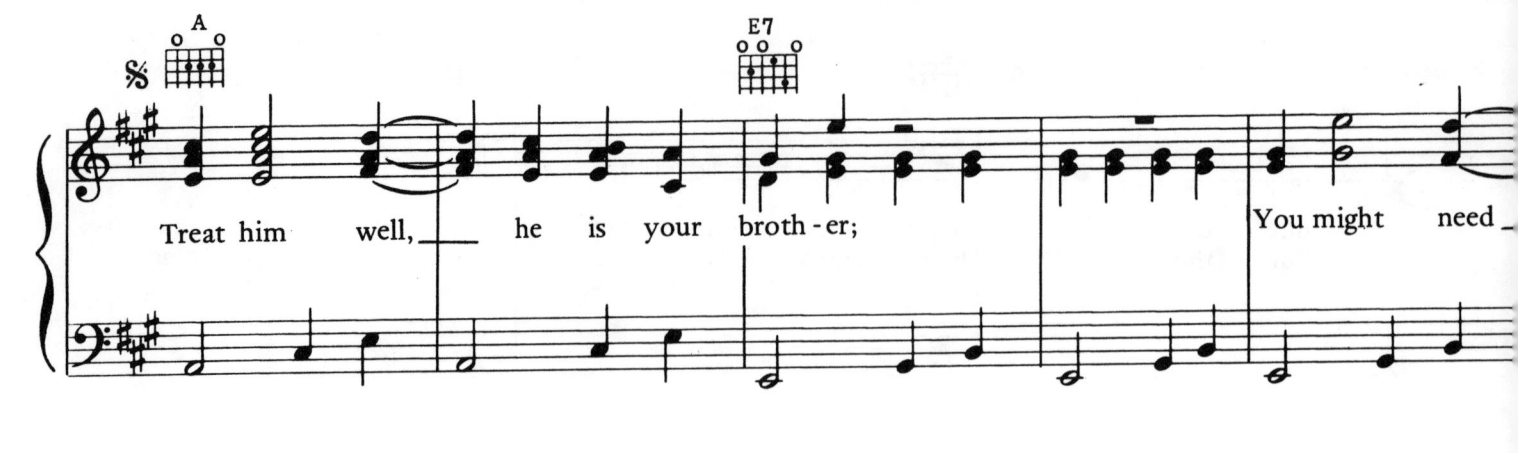

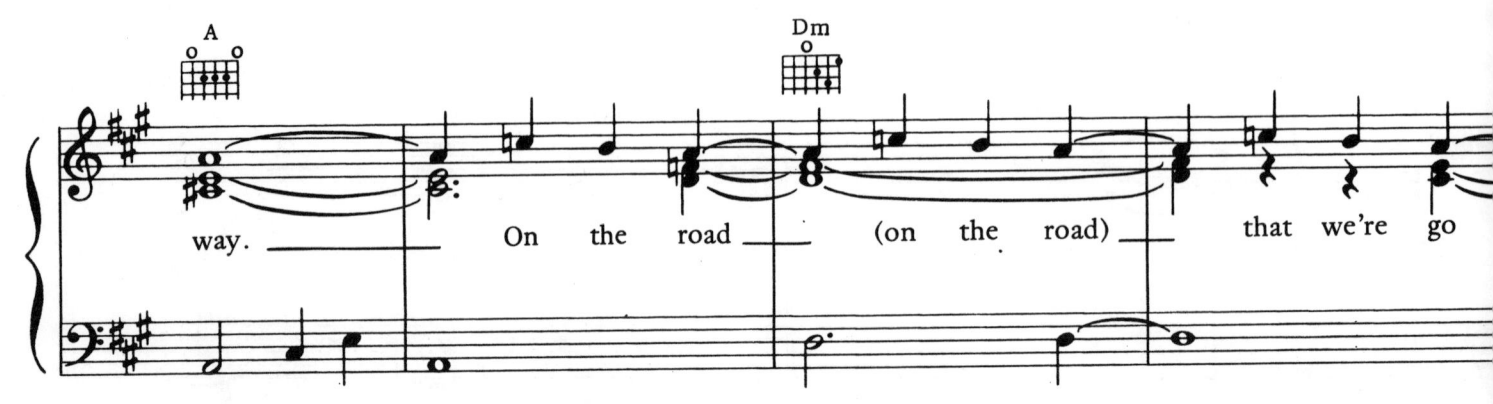

Hey, Hey Helen

Words and Music by
Benny Andersson & Björn Ulvae[us]

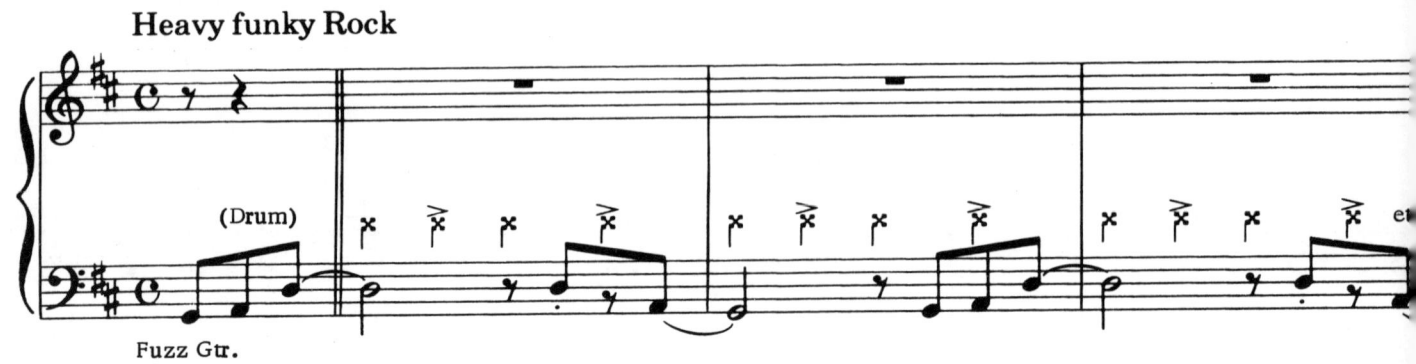

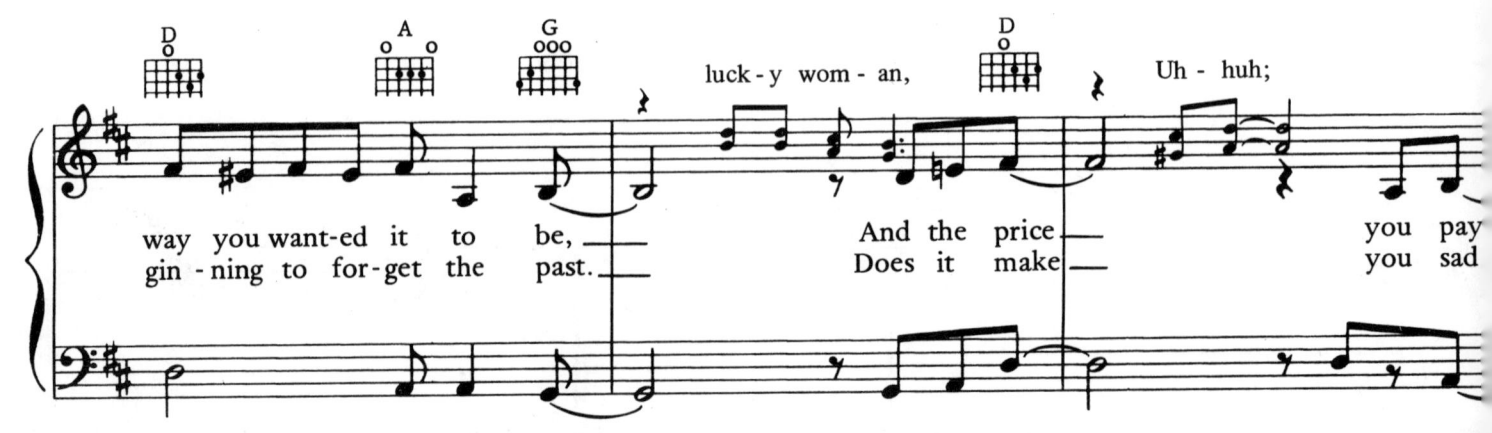

Hole In Your Soul

Words and Music by
Benny Andersson & Björn Ulvaeus

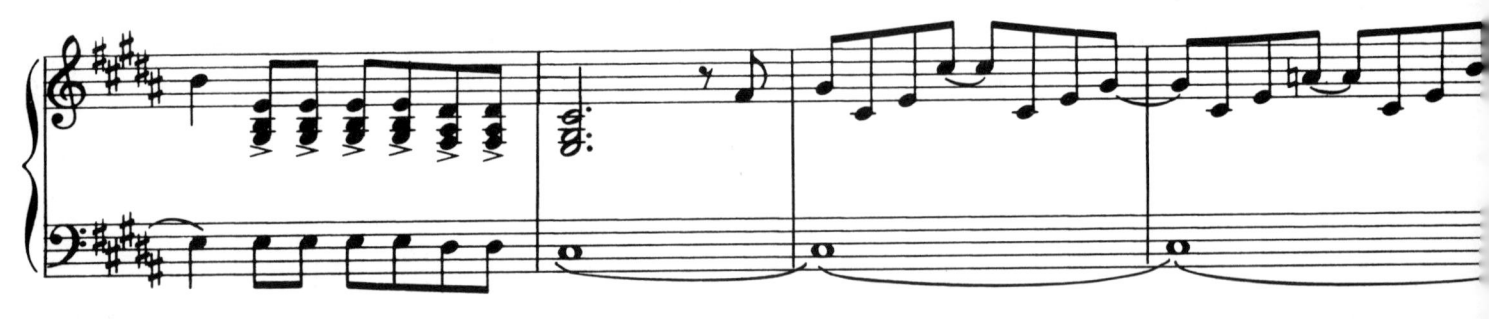

Copyright © 1977, 1978 Union Songs AB, Stockholm, Sweden for the world
Countless Songs Ltd. for U.S.A. and Canada
International Copyright Secured   All Rights Reserved

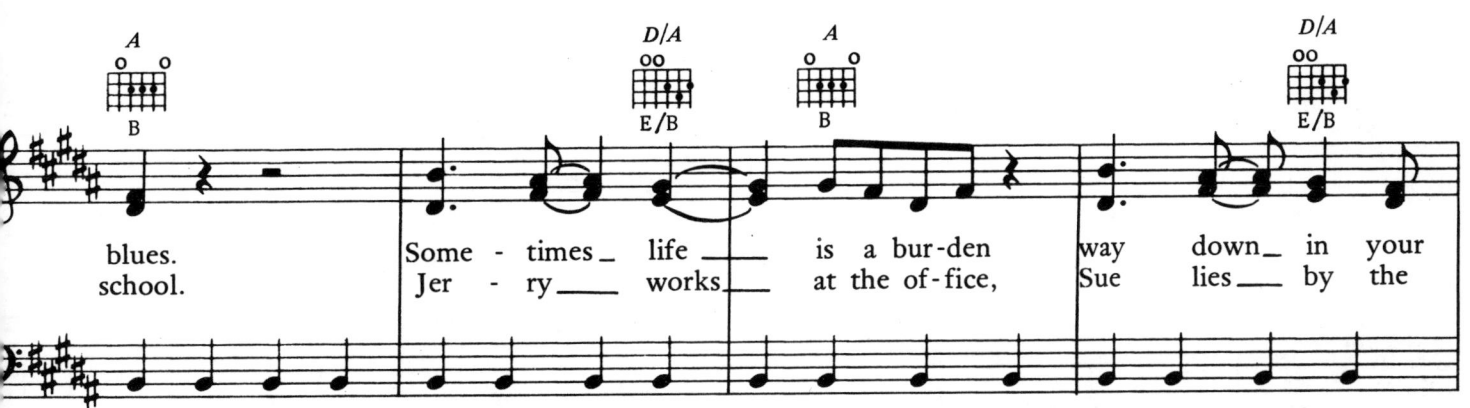
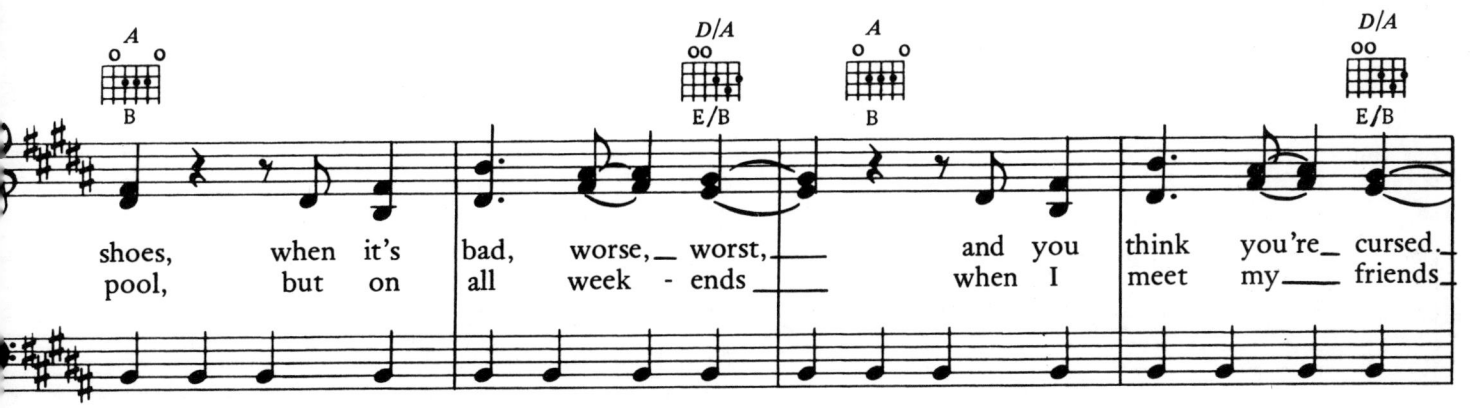
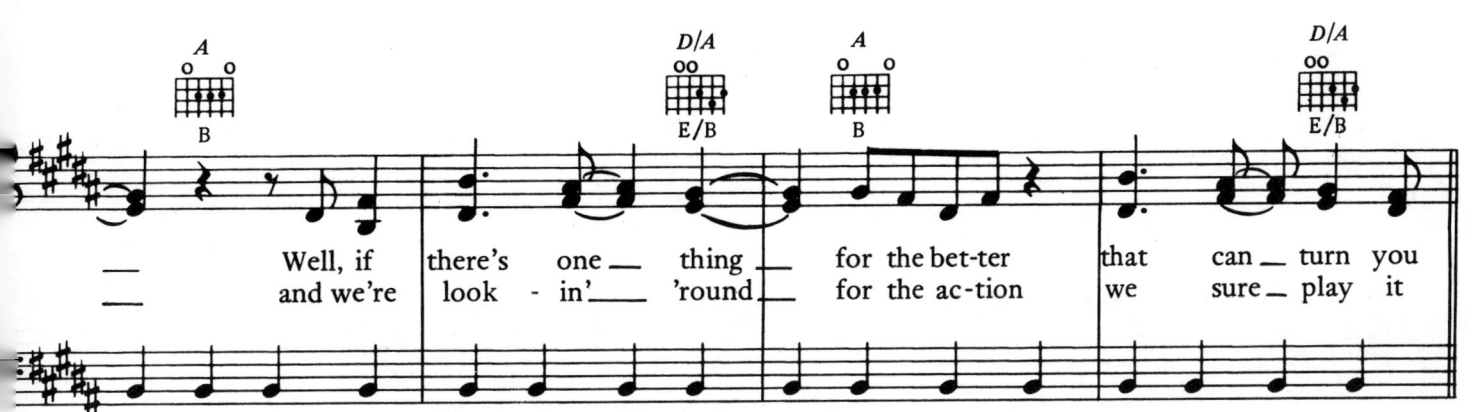

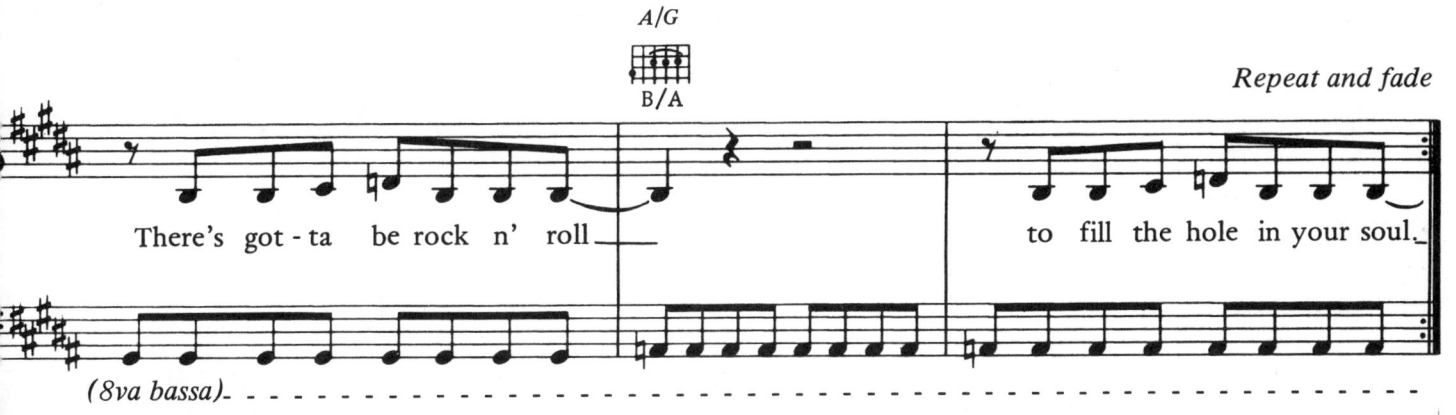

Repeat and fade

95

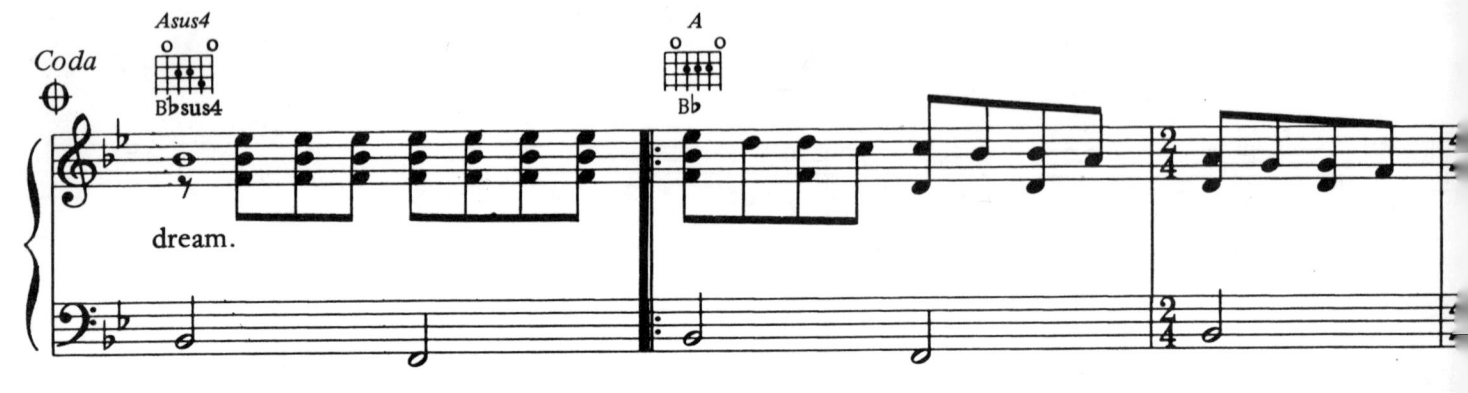
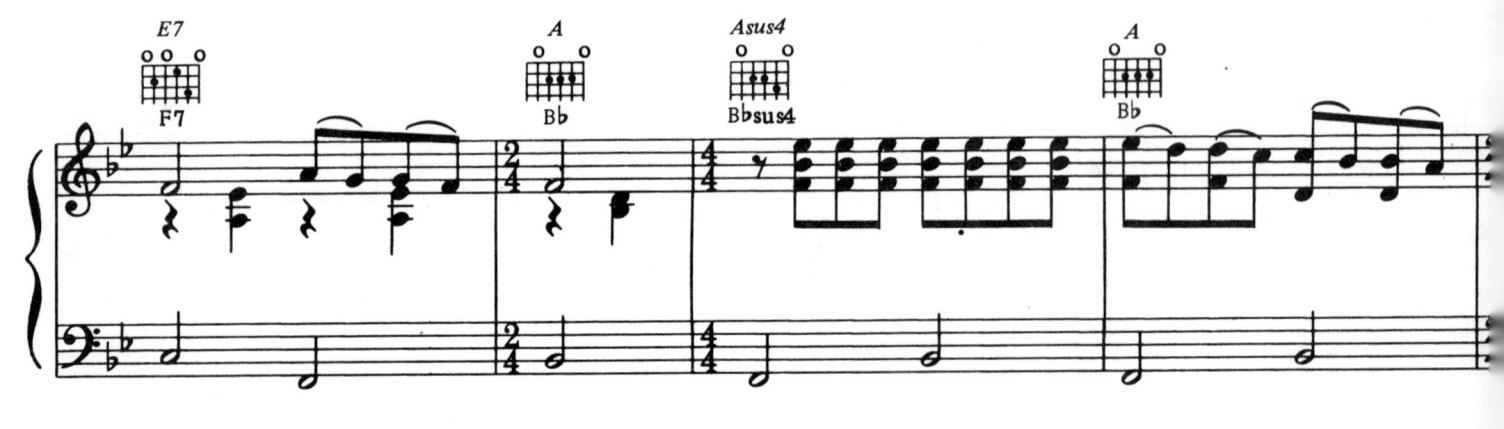

I Do, I Do, I Do, I Do, I Do

Words and Music by
Benny Andersson, Björn Ulvaeus
and Stig Anderson

Love me or leave me, make your choice; But believe me, I love

you, I do, I do, I do, I do, I do.

Copyright © 1975 Union Songs AB, Stockholm, Sweden for the world
Countless Songs Ltd. for U.S.A. and Canada
International Copyright Secured   All Rights Reserved

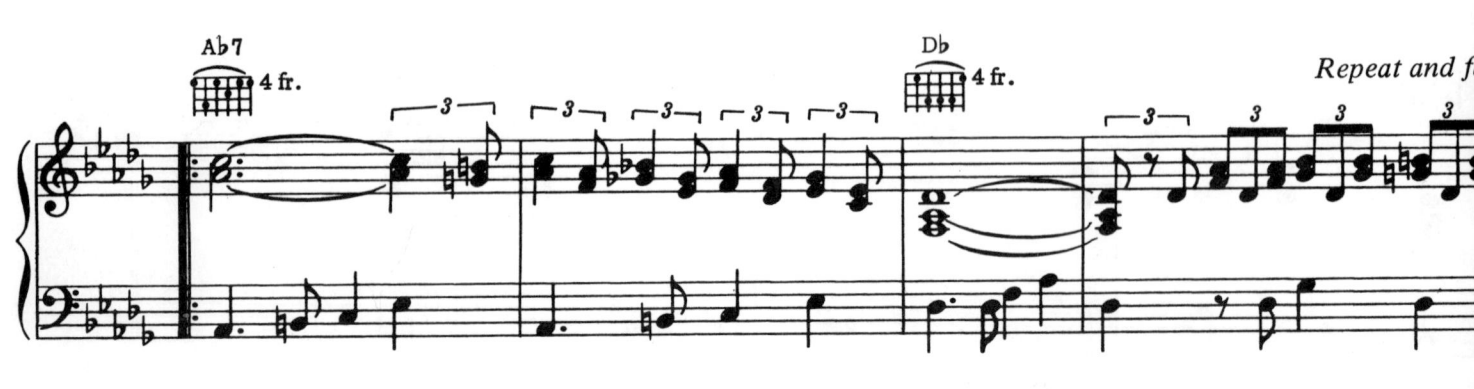

I Wonder (Departure)

Words and Music by
Benny Andersson, Björn Ulvaeus
and Stig Anderson

Copyright © 1977, 1978 Polar Music AB, Stockholm, Sweden for the world
Artwork Music Co., Inc. for U.S.A. and Canada
International Copyright Secured   All Rights Reserved

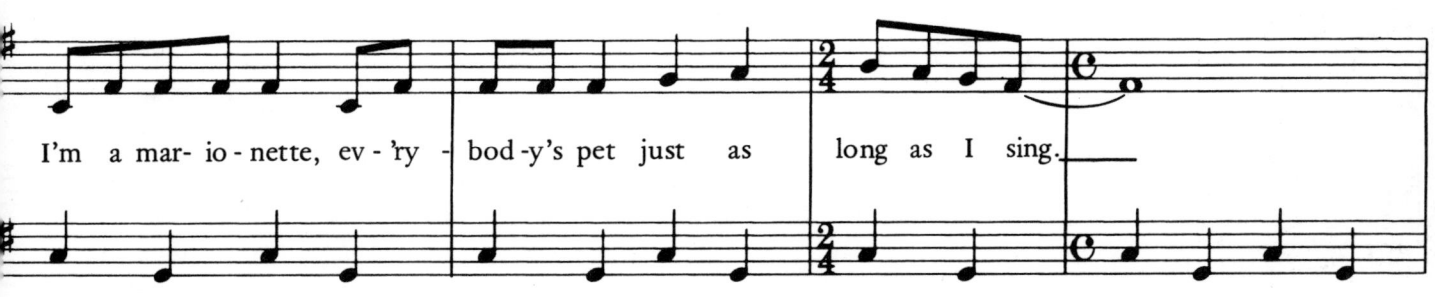

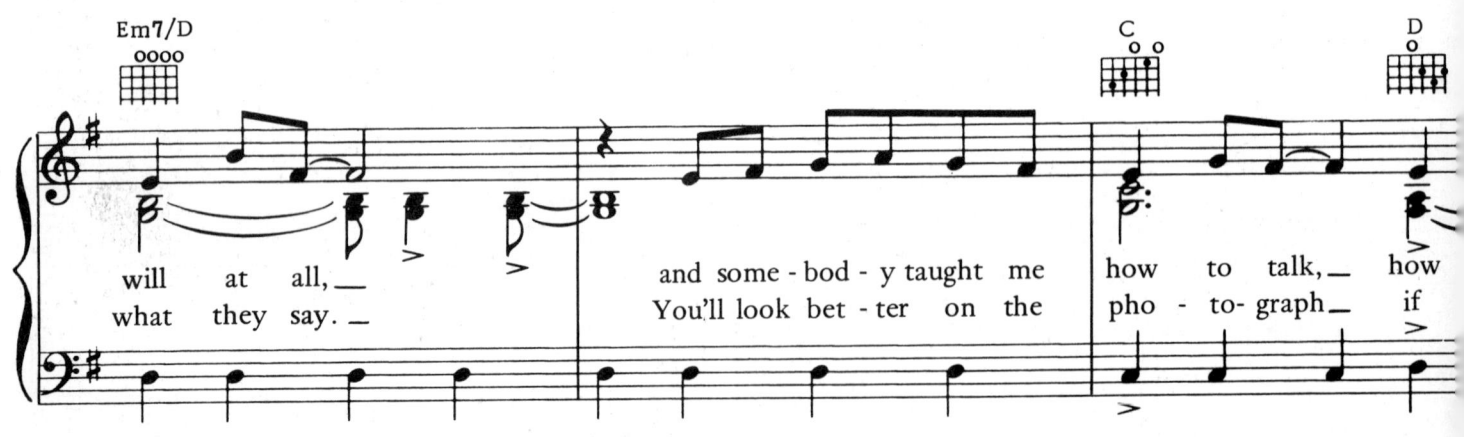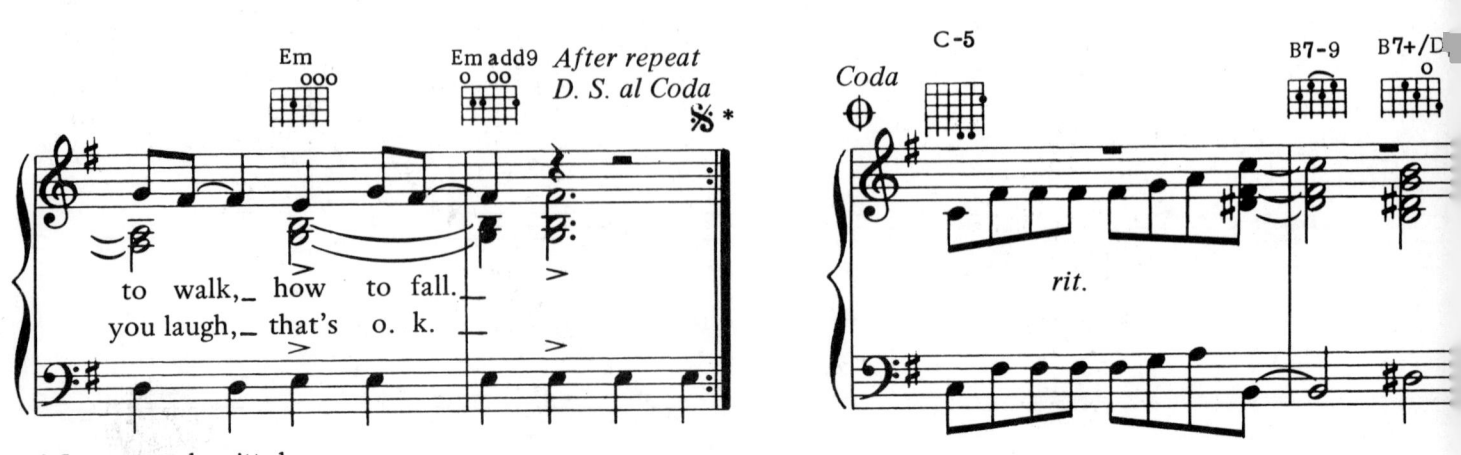

*Instrumental omitted

Slow

You're so free, — that's what ev-'ry-bod-y's tell-ing me. — Yet I feel I'm like an out-ward bound, pushed a-round ref-u-gee.

If It Wasn't For The Nights

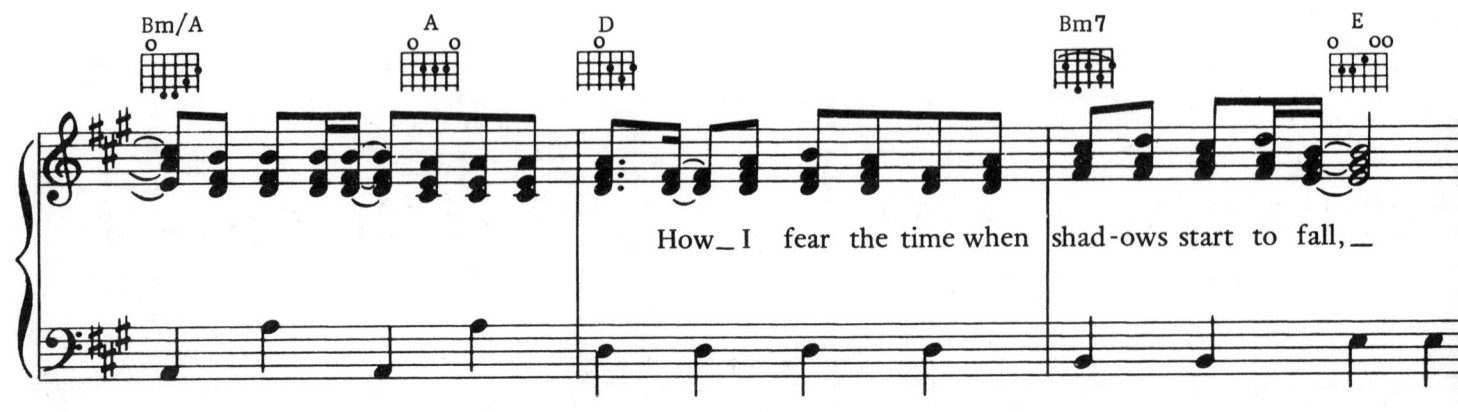

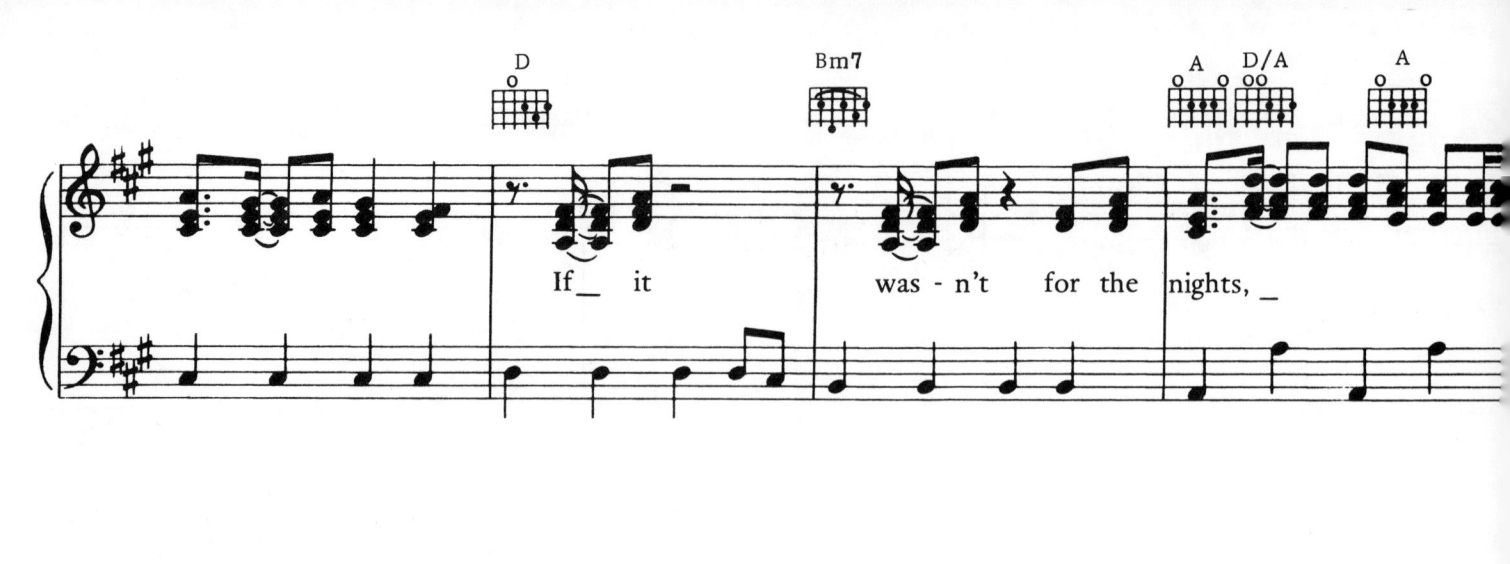

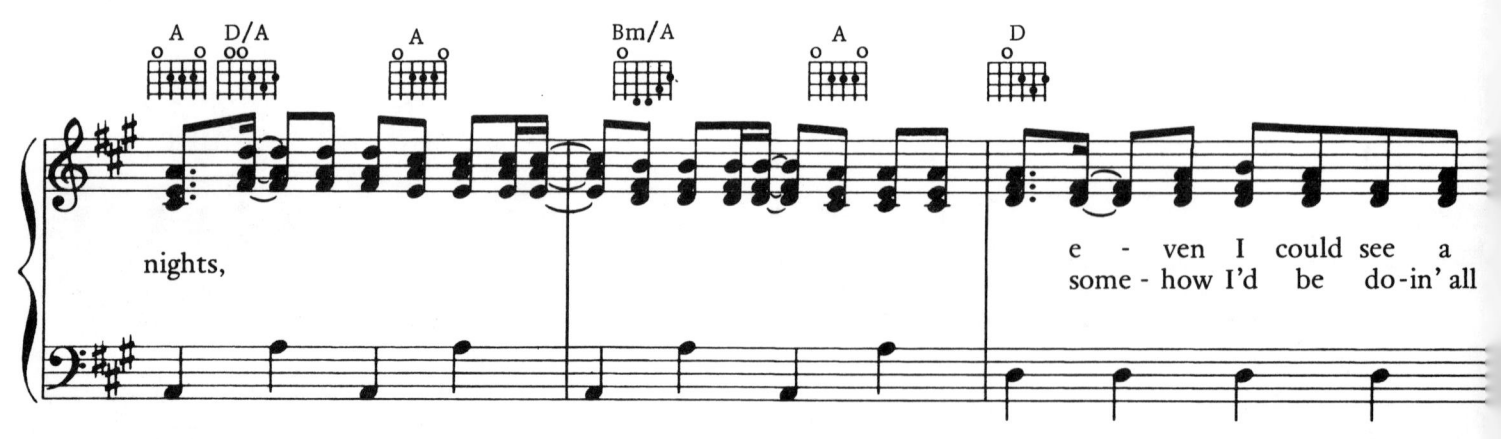

Intermezzo No. 1

Music by
Benny Andersson & Björn Ulvaeus

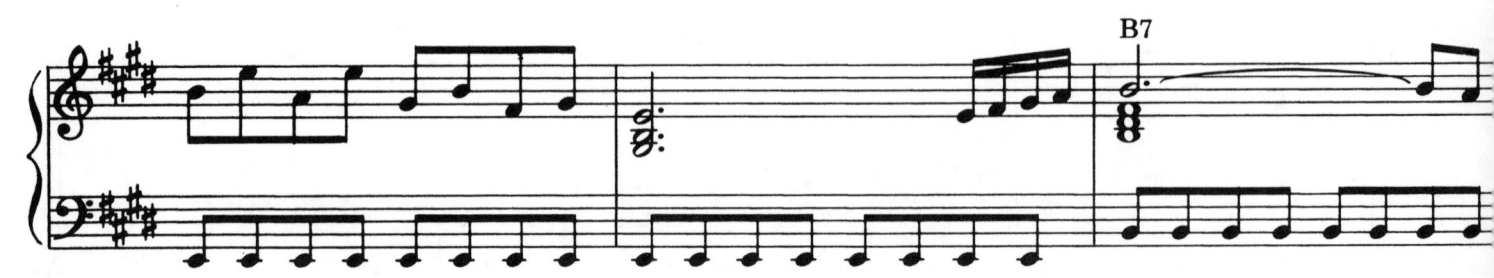

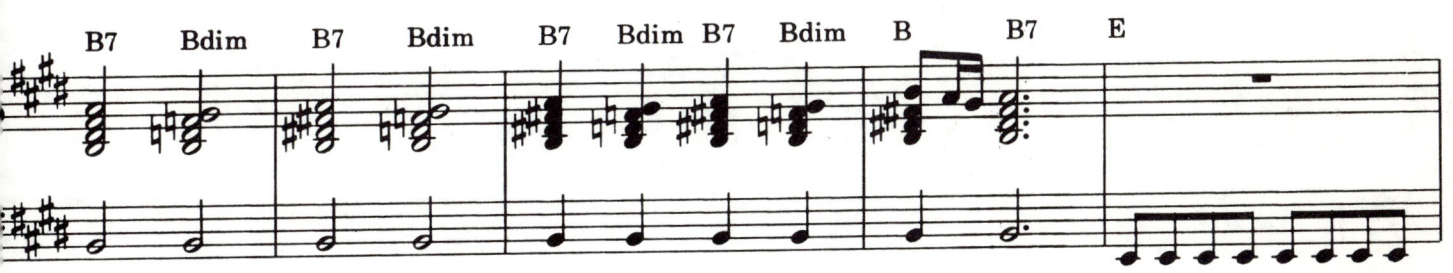

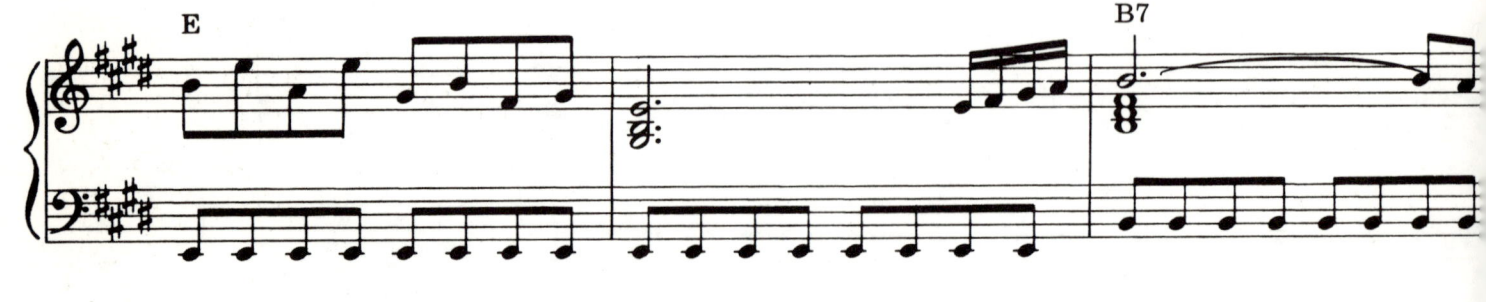

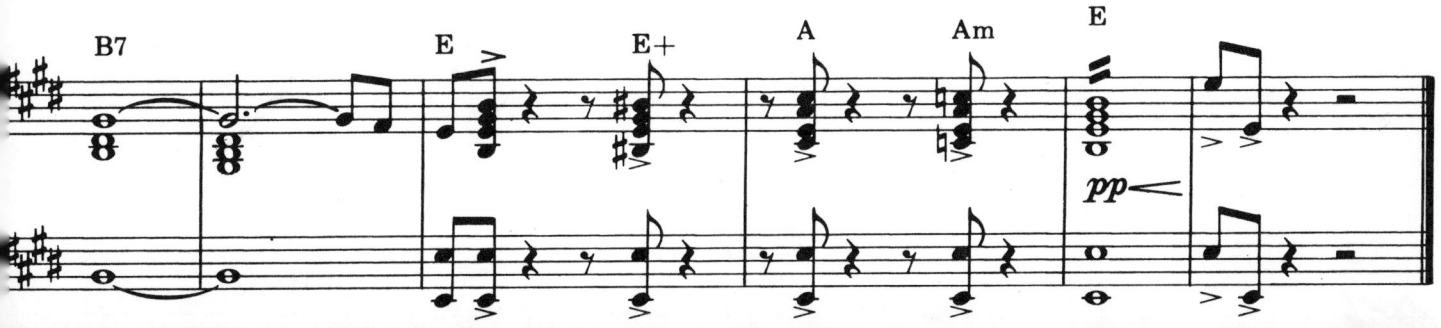

Kisses Of Fire

Words and Music by
Benny Andersson & Björn Ulvaeus

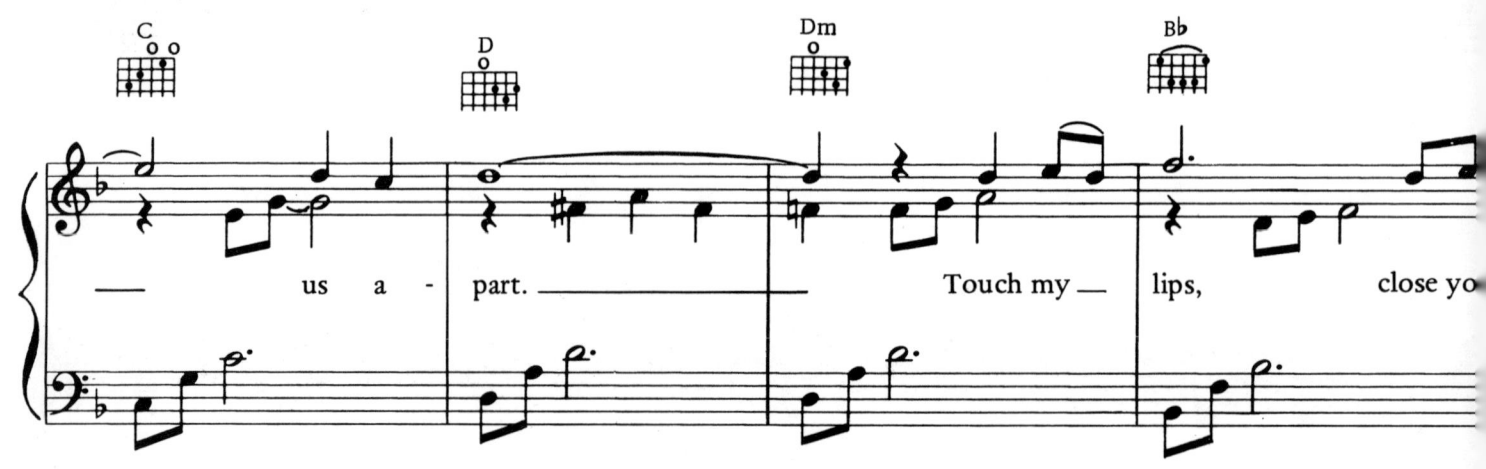

Copyright © 1979 Union Songs AB, Stockholm, Sweden for the world
Artwork Music Co., Inc. for U.S.A. and Canada
International Copyright Secured   All Rights Reserved

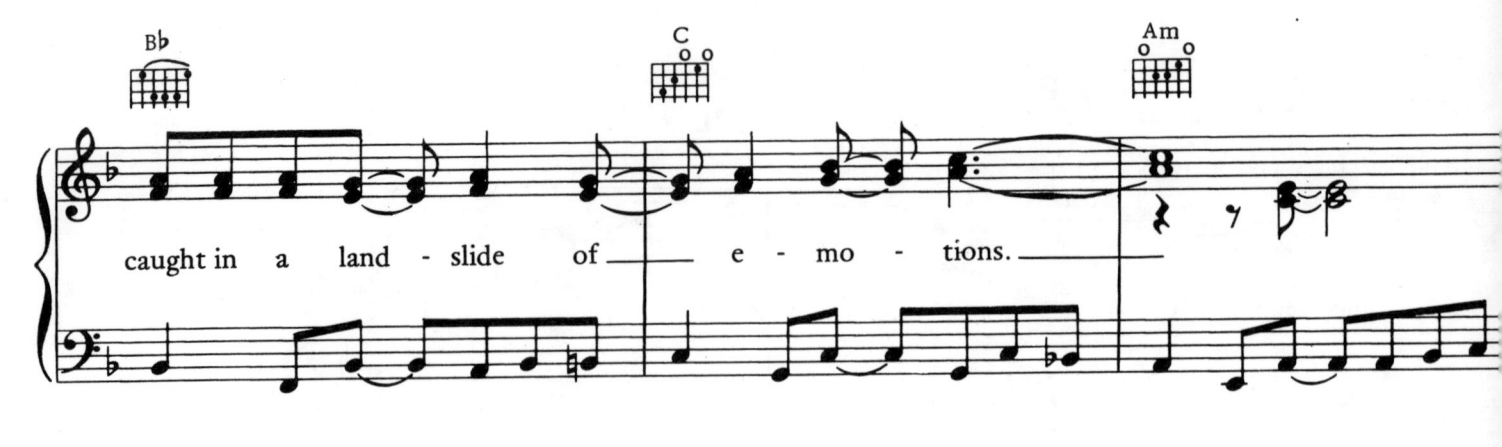

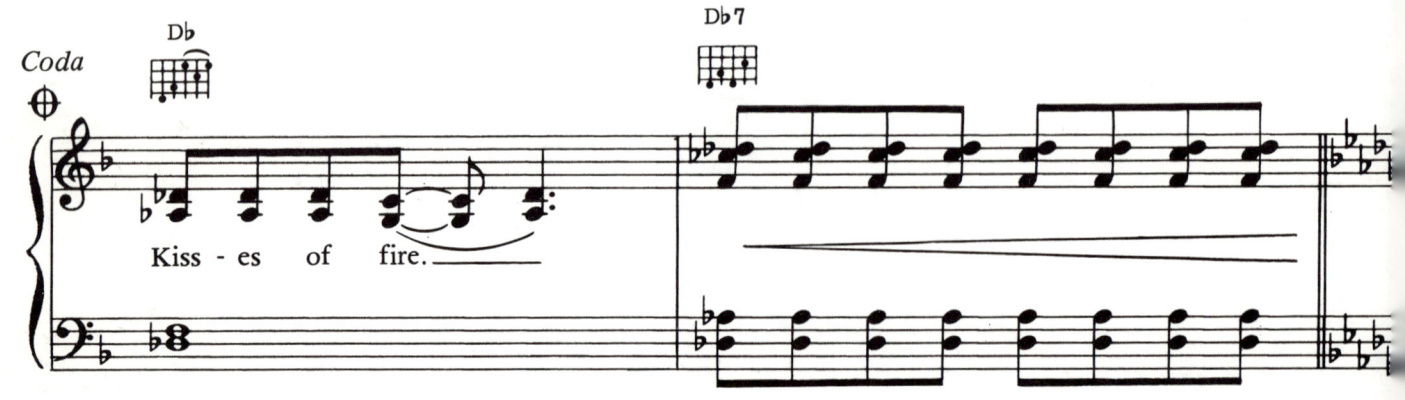

Mamma Mia

Words and Music by
Benny Andersson, Björn Ulvae
and Stig Anderson

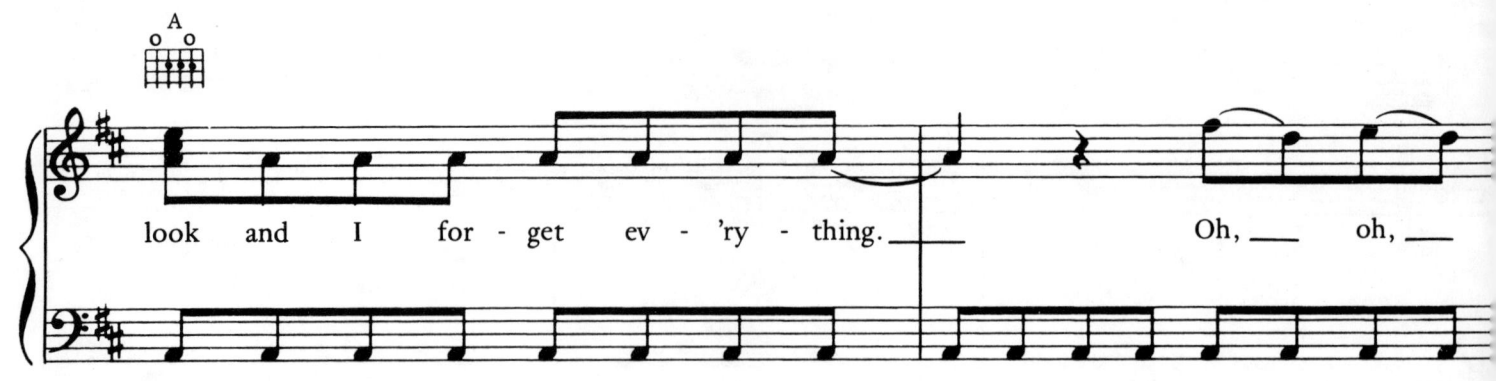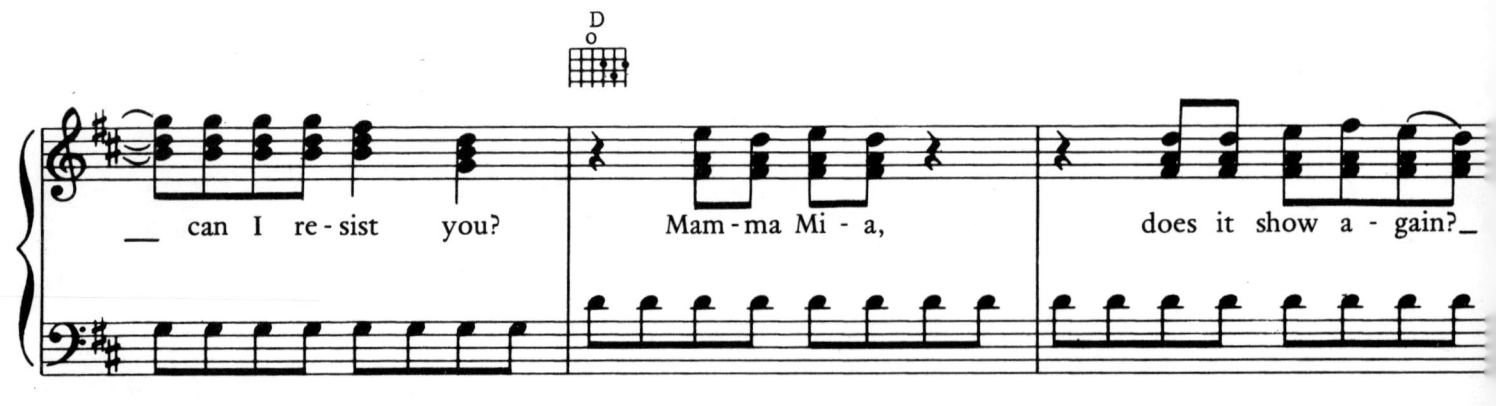

The King Has Lost His Crown

Words and Music by
Benny Andersson & Björn Ulvaeus

Copyright © 1979 Union Songs AB, Stockholm, Sweden for the world
Countless Songs Ltd. for U.S.A. and Canada
International Copyright Secured   All Rights Reserved

The world is up - side down, the
Em
E
Repeat and fade
king has lost his crown.
Dis - as - ter and dis -

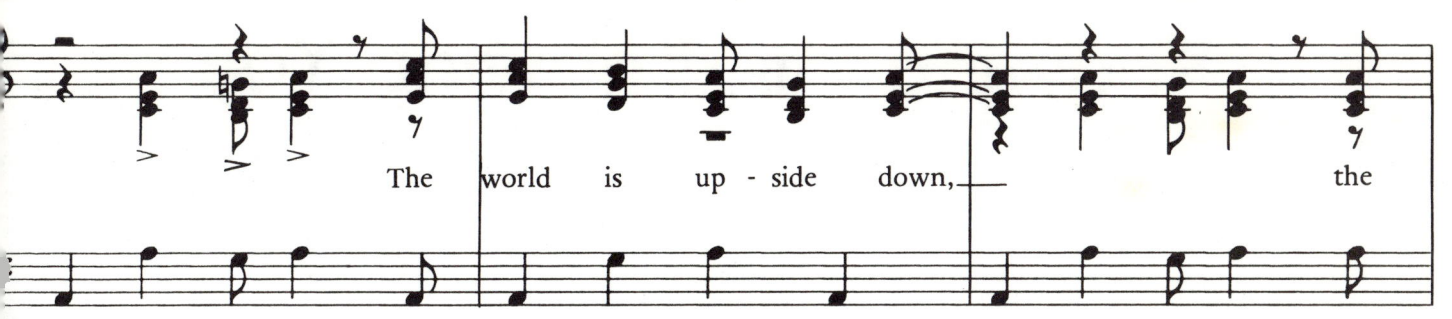

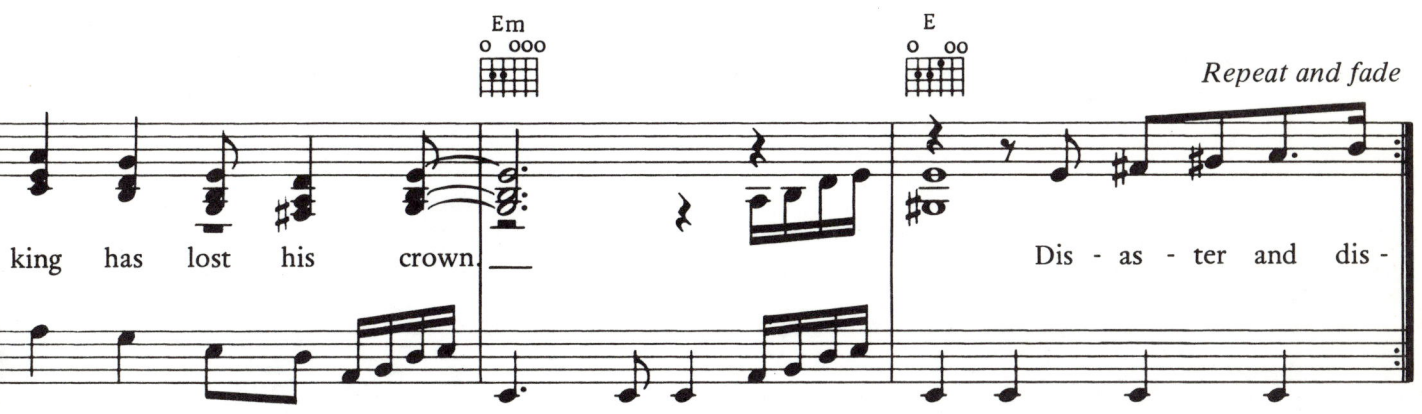

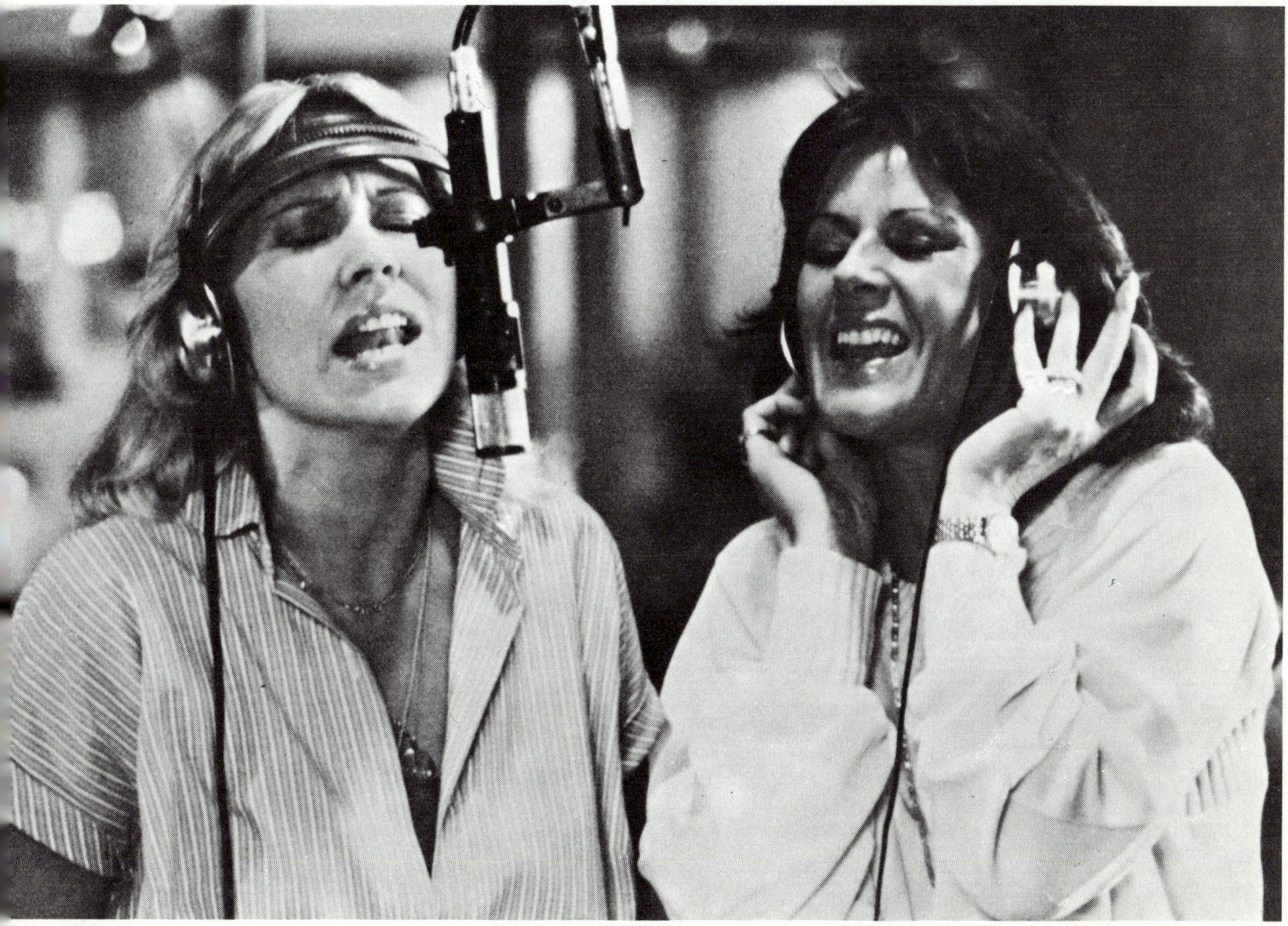

Knowing Me, Knowing You

Words and Music by
Benny Andersson, Björn Ulvaeus
and Stig Anderson

Copyright © 1976, Polar Music AB, Stockholm, Sweden for the world
Countless Songs Ltd. for U.S.A. and Canada
International Copyright Secured   All Rights Reserved

D. S. al Coda
A
Bm
A
Bm
G
Know-ing me, know-ing
D
Bm
F♯m
G
A
Repeat and fade
do.

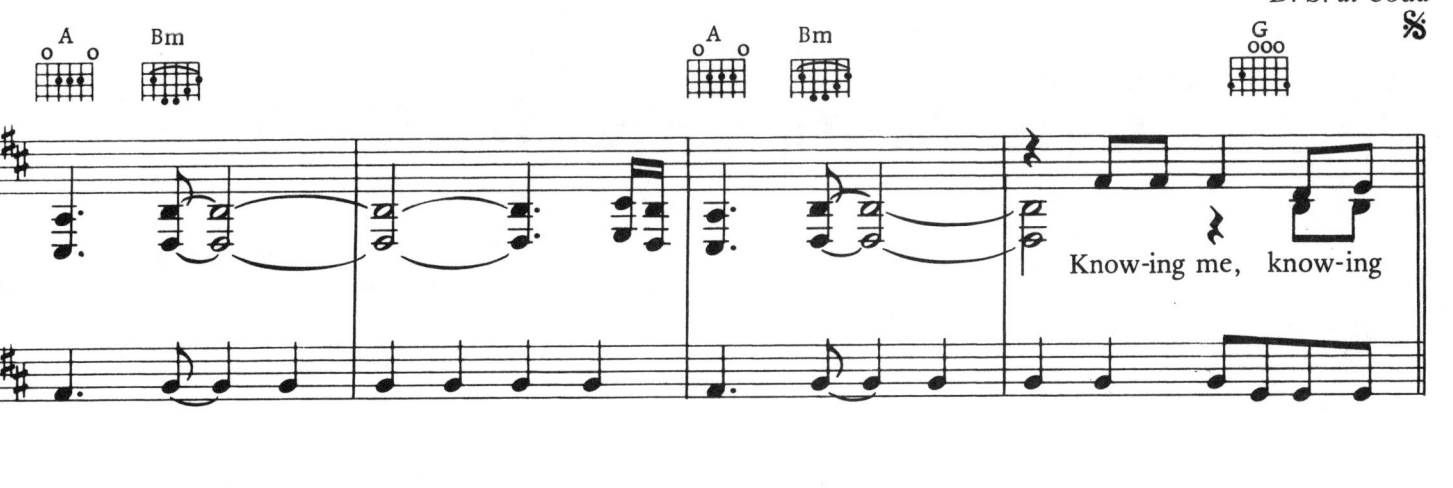

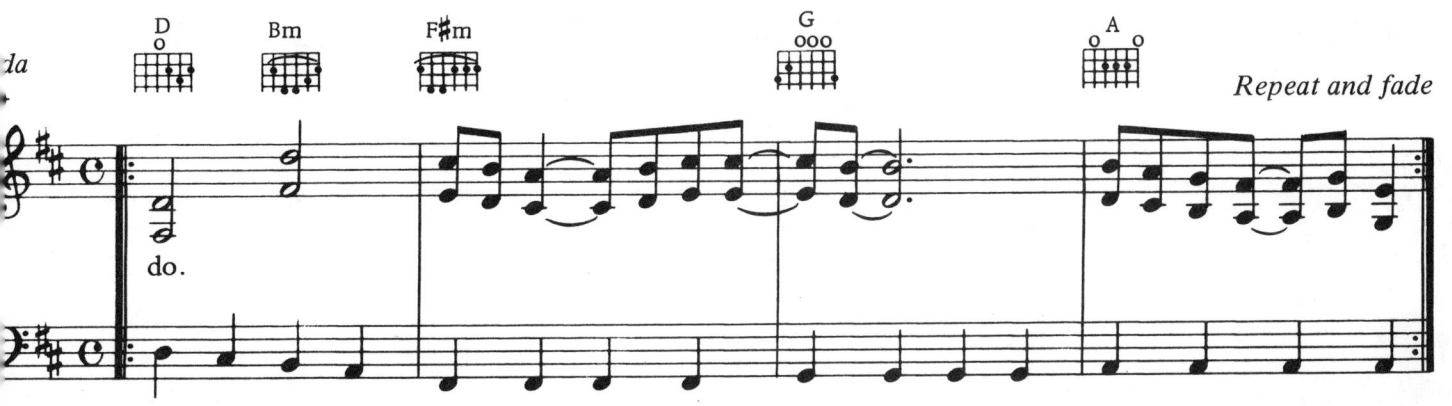

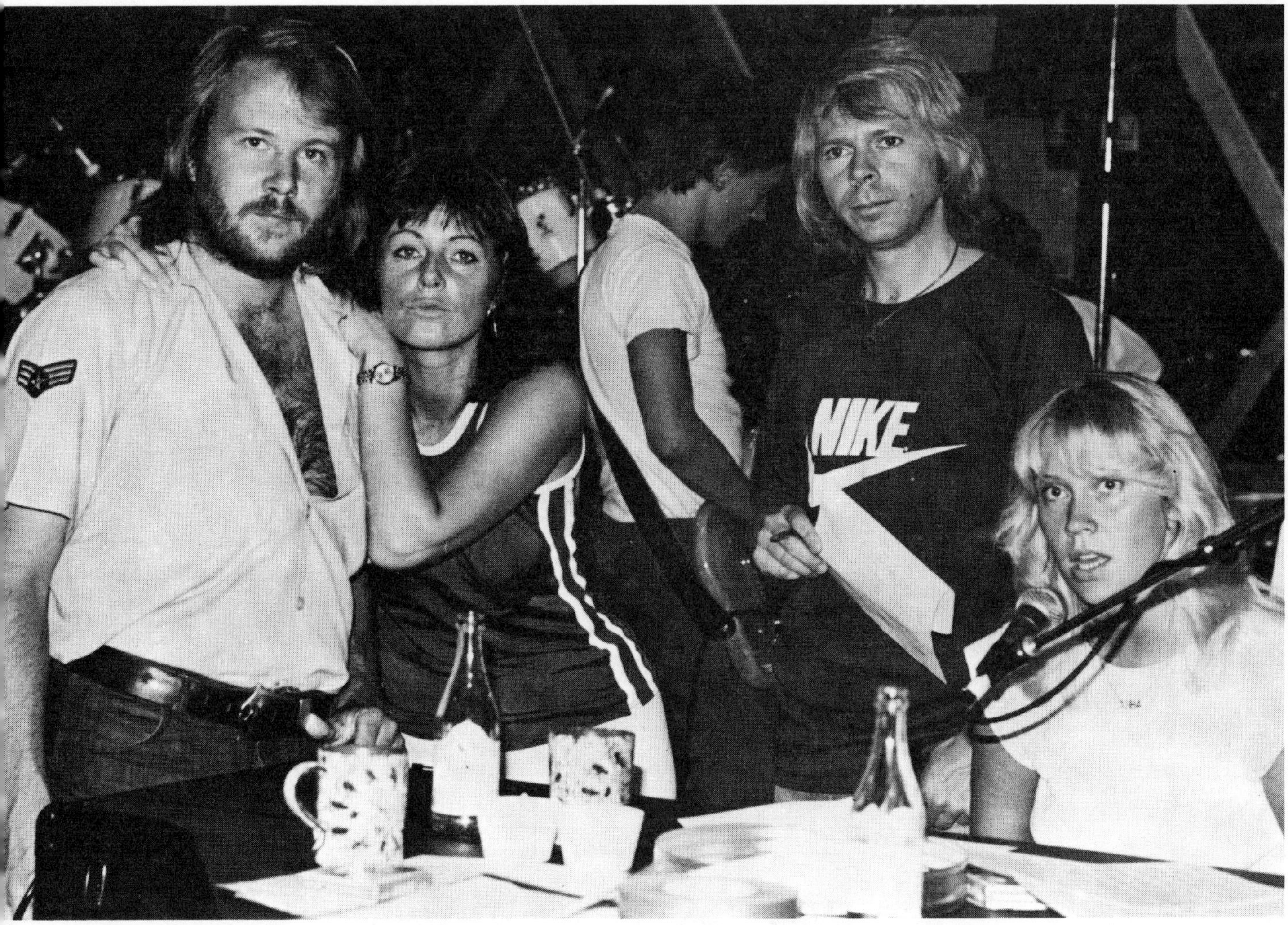

One Man, One Woman

Words and Music by
Benny Andersson & Björn Ulvaeus

Slow and steady, in 2 ($\quarternote = 1$ beat)

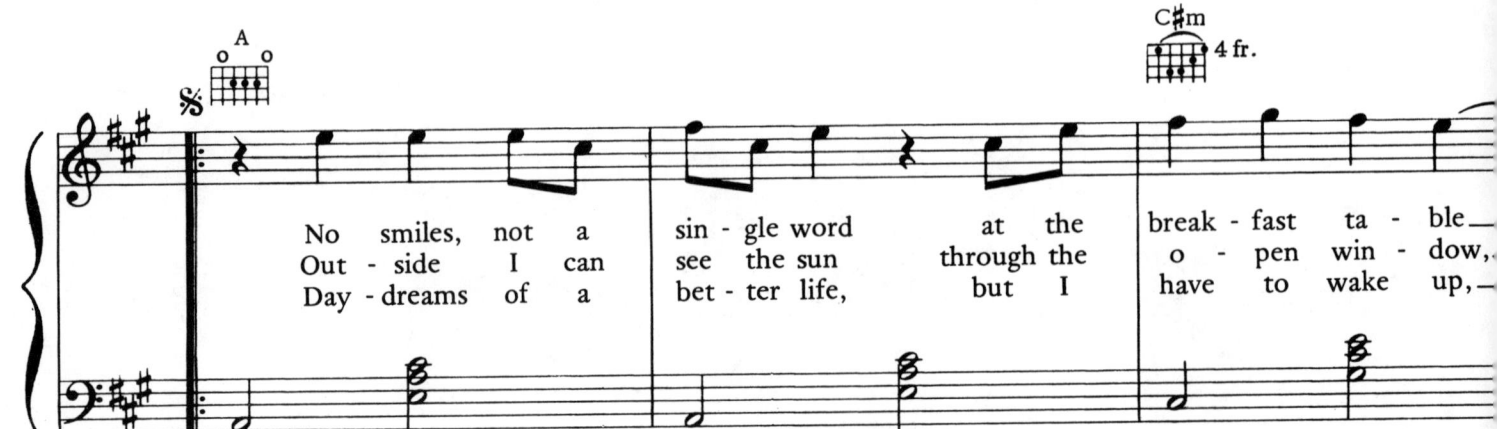

No smiles, not a sin-gle word at the break-fast ta-ble
Out-side I can see the sun through the o-pen win-dow,
Day-dreams of a bet-ter life, but I have to wake up,

Copyright © 1977, 1978 Union Songs AB, Stockholm, Sweden for the world
Countless Songs Ltd. for U.S.A. and Canada
International Copyright Secured   All Rights Reserved

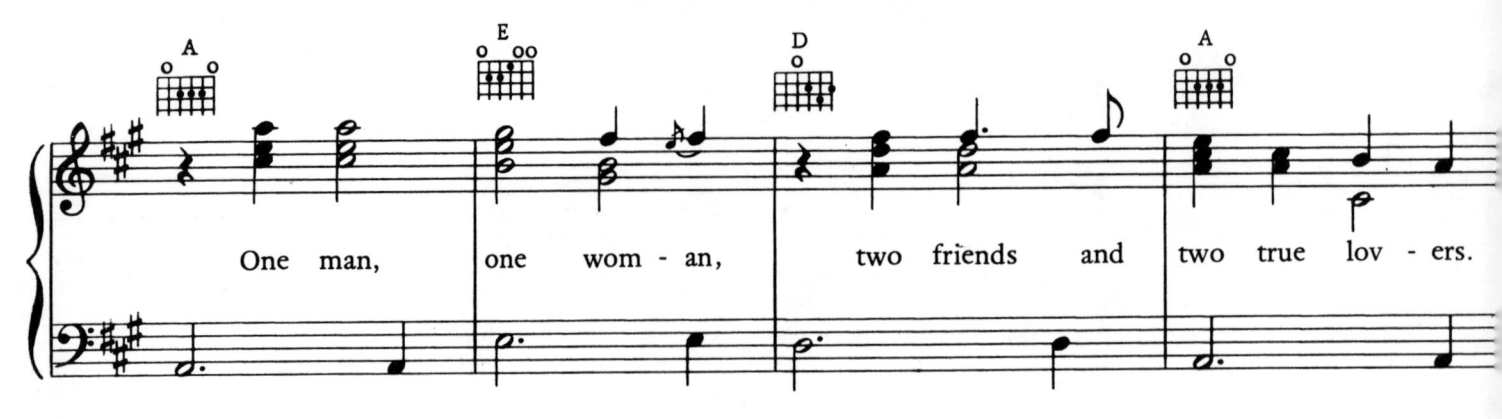
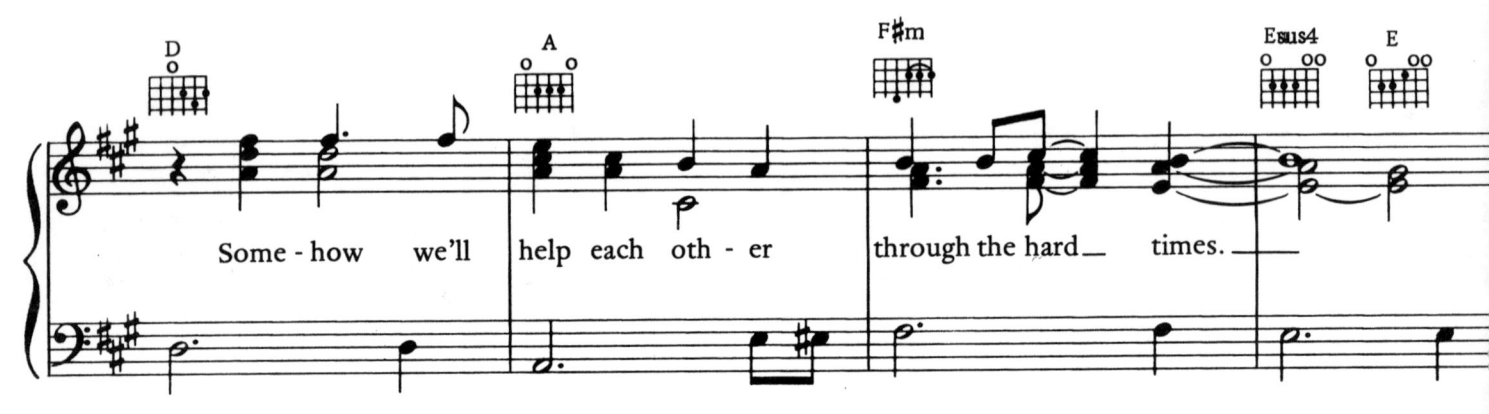
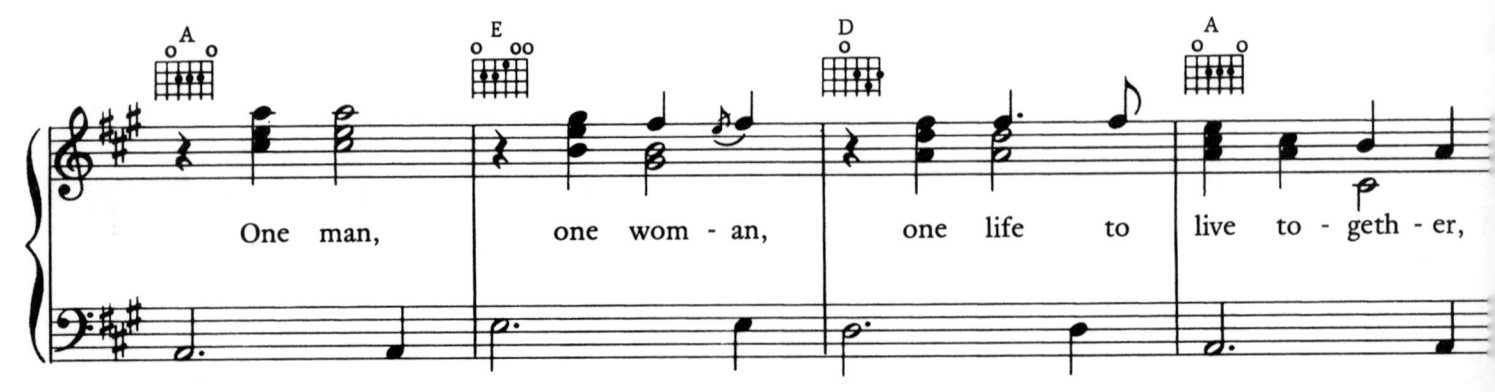

King Kong Song

Words and Music by
Benny Andersson & Björn Ulvaeus

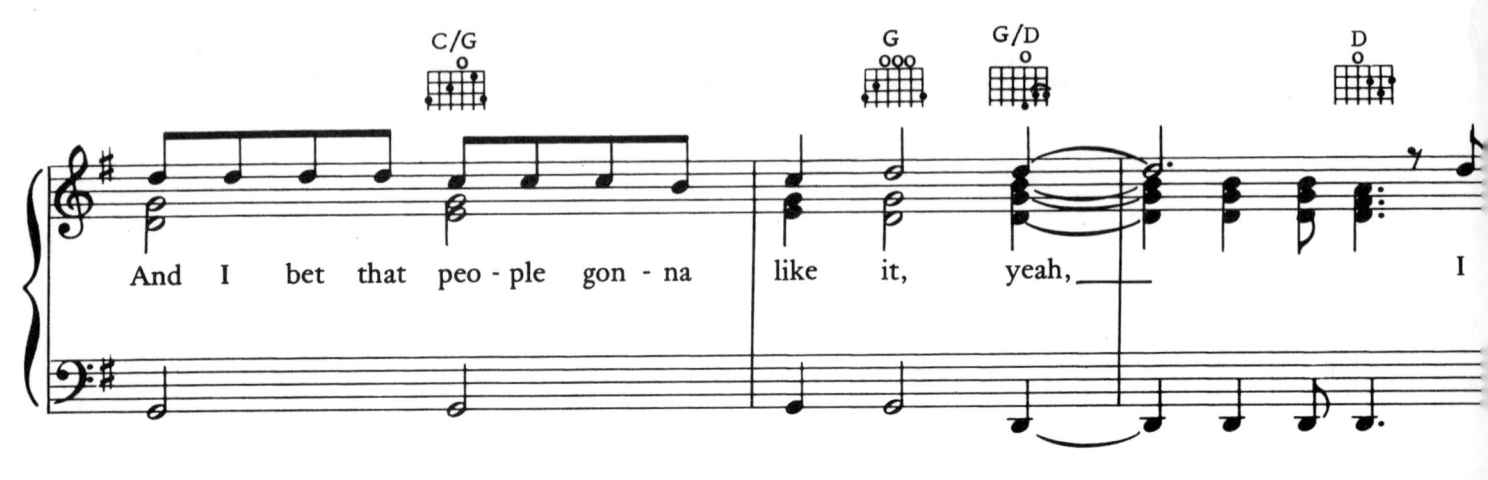
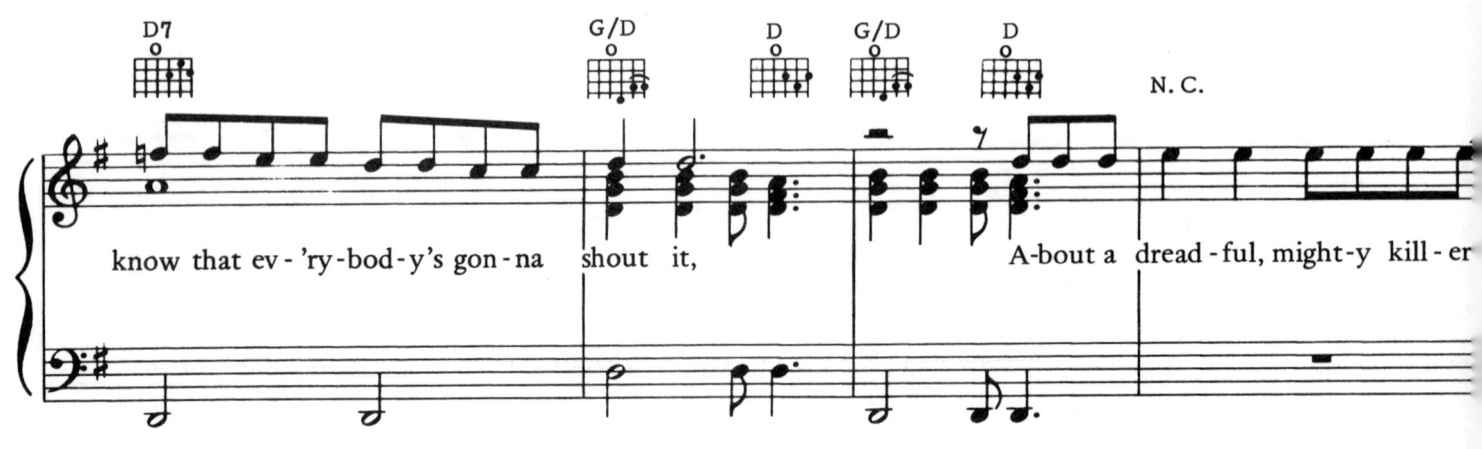

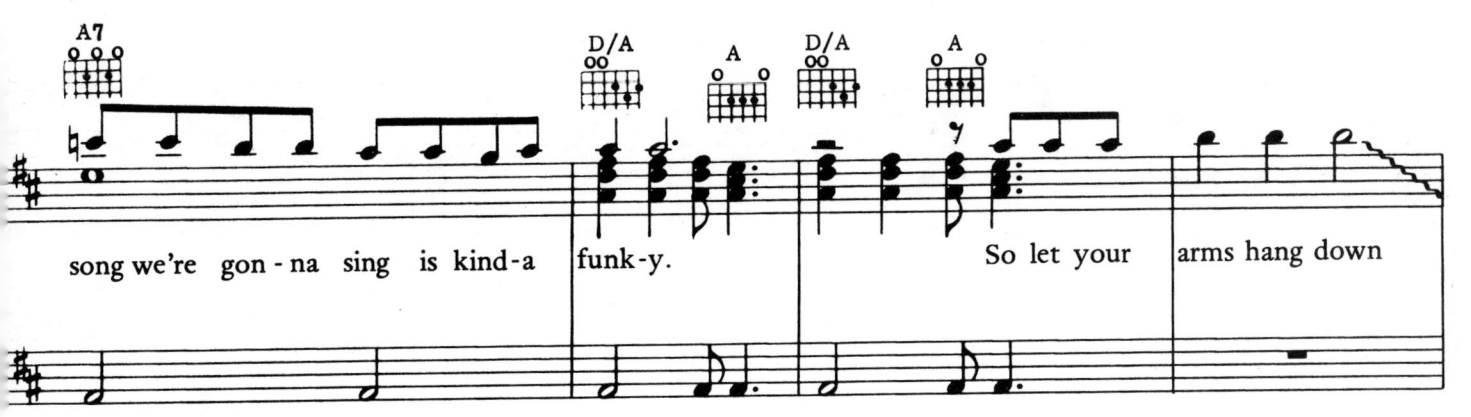

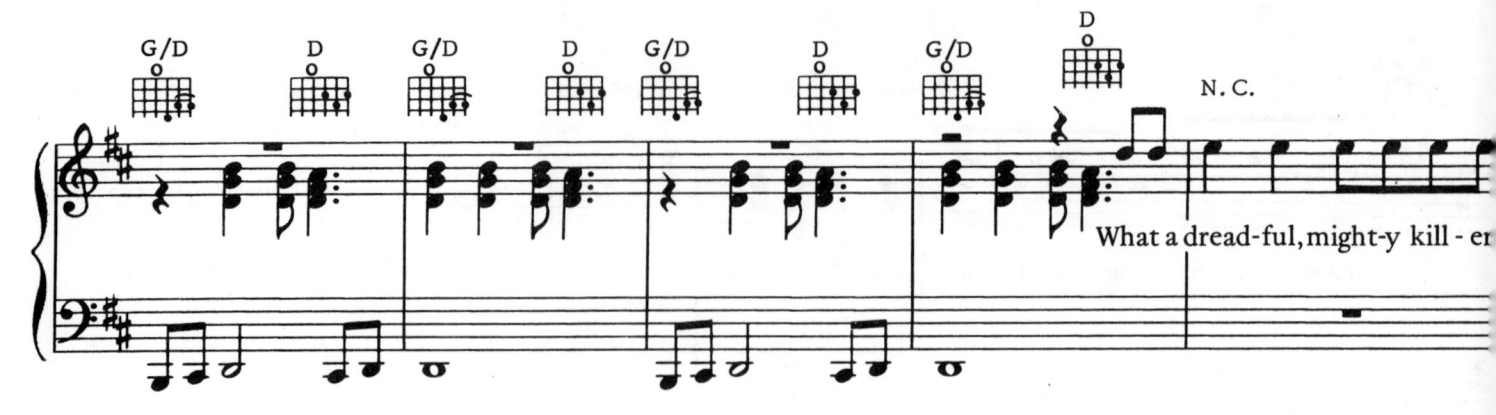
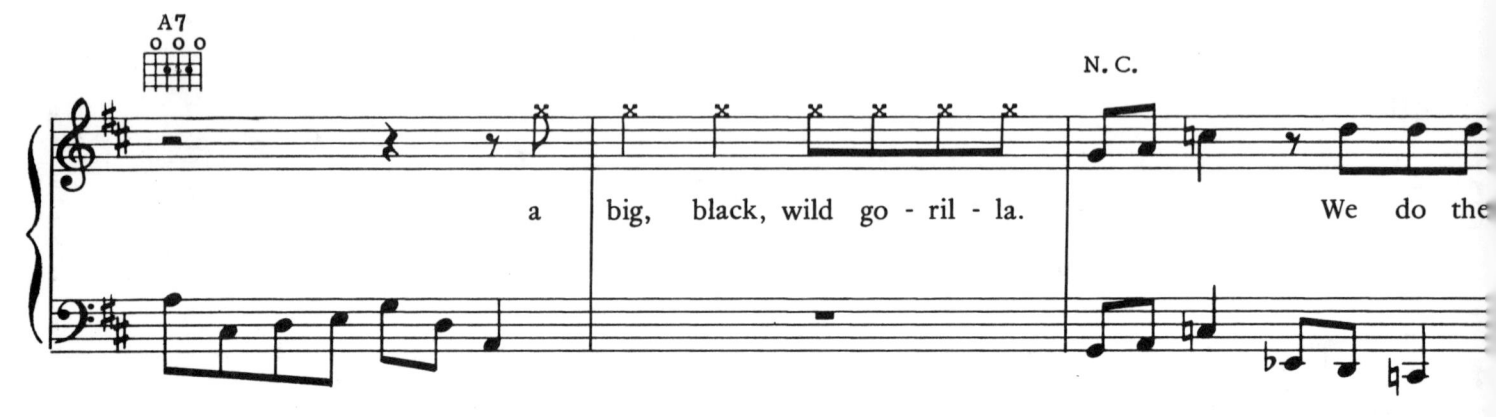
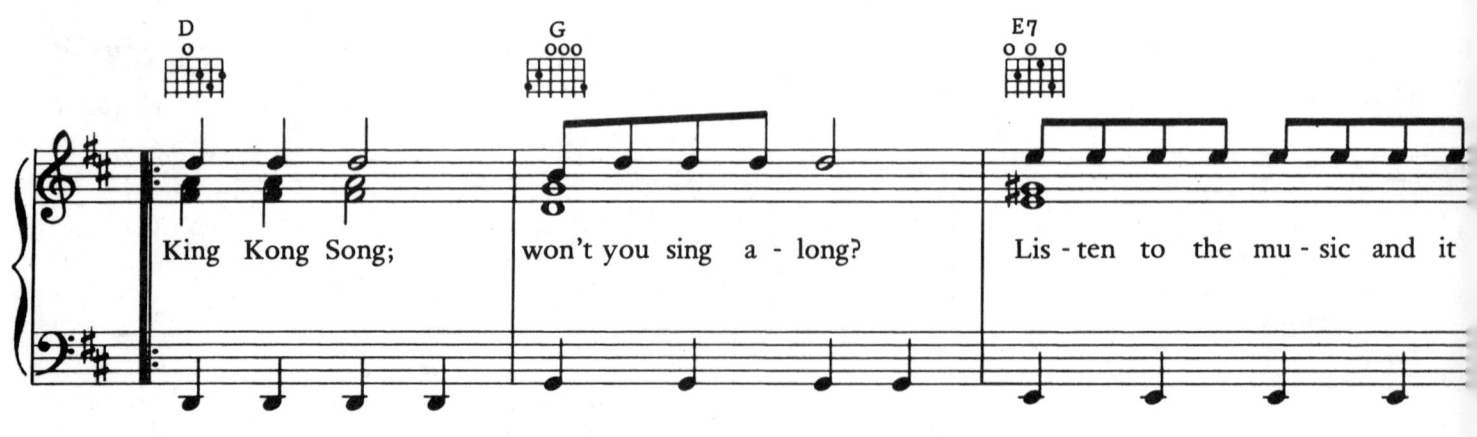
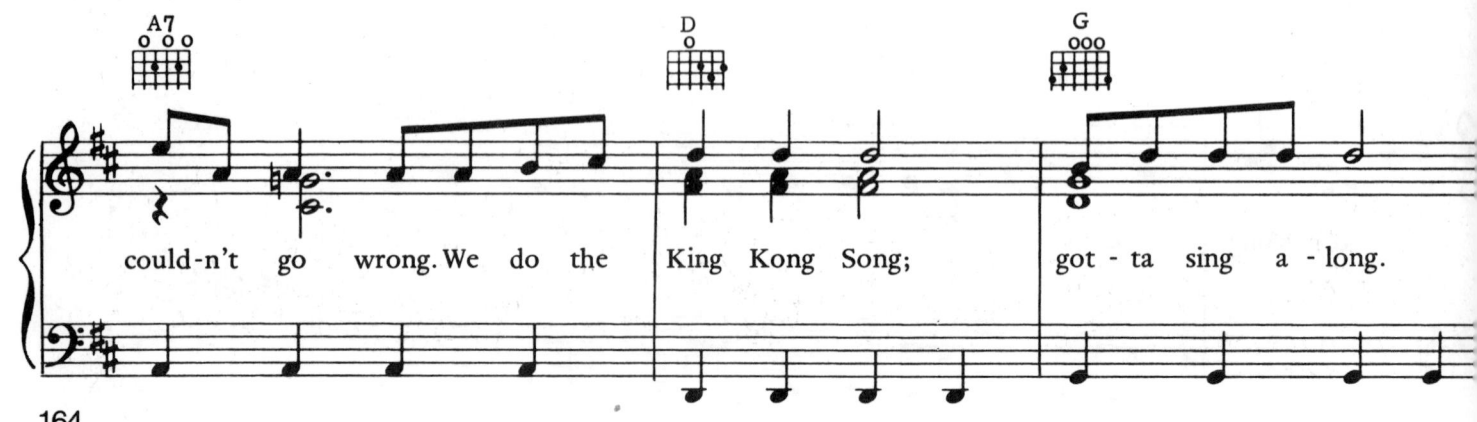

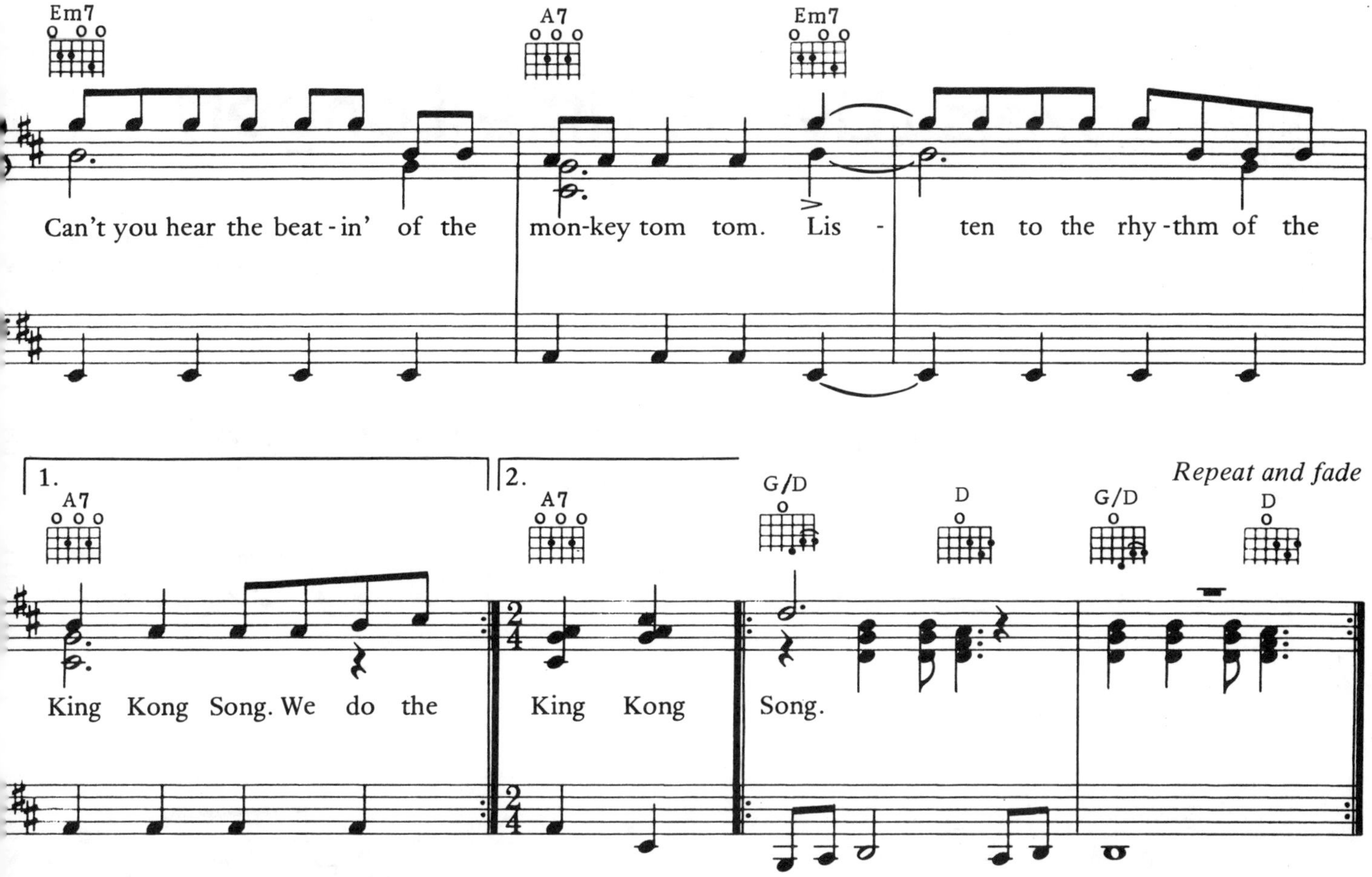
Em7
A7
Em7
Can't you hear the beat-in' of the mon-key tom tom. Lis - ten to the rhy-thm of the
1.
A7
2.
A7
G/D
D
G/D
D
Repeat and fade
King Kong Song. We do the King Kong Song.

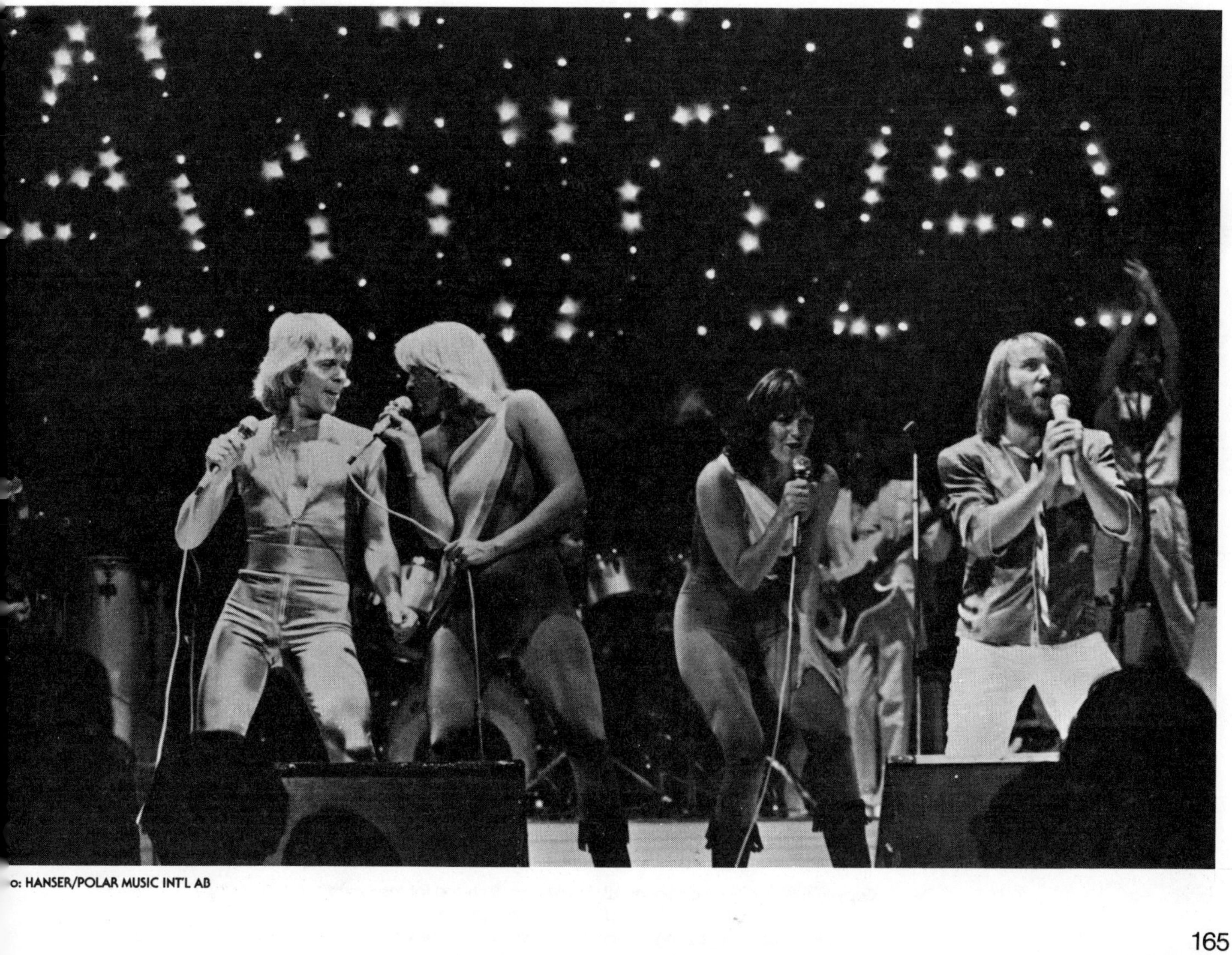
o: HANSER/POLAR MUSIC INT'L AB

Lovers (Live A Little Longer)

Words and Music by
Benny Andersson & Björn Ulvae

Disco (in 2, ♩=1 beat)

Copyright © 1979 Union Songs AB, Stockholm, Sweden for the world
Artwork Music Co., Inc. for U.S.A. and Canada
International Copyright Secured   All Rights Reserved

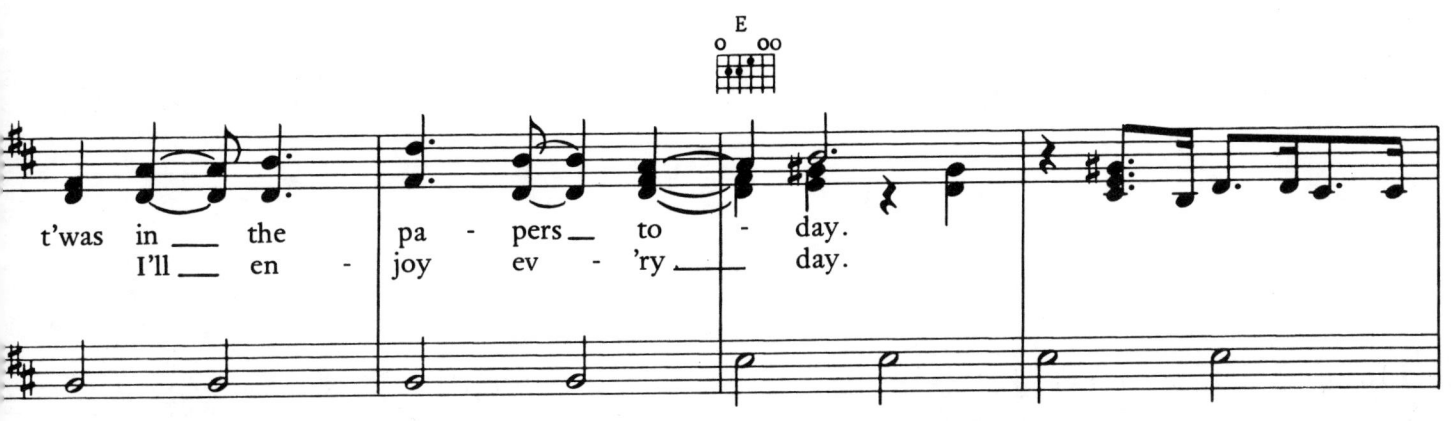

HANSER/POLAR MUSIC INT'L AB

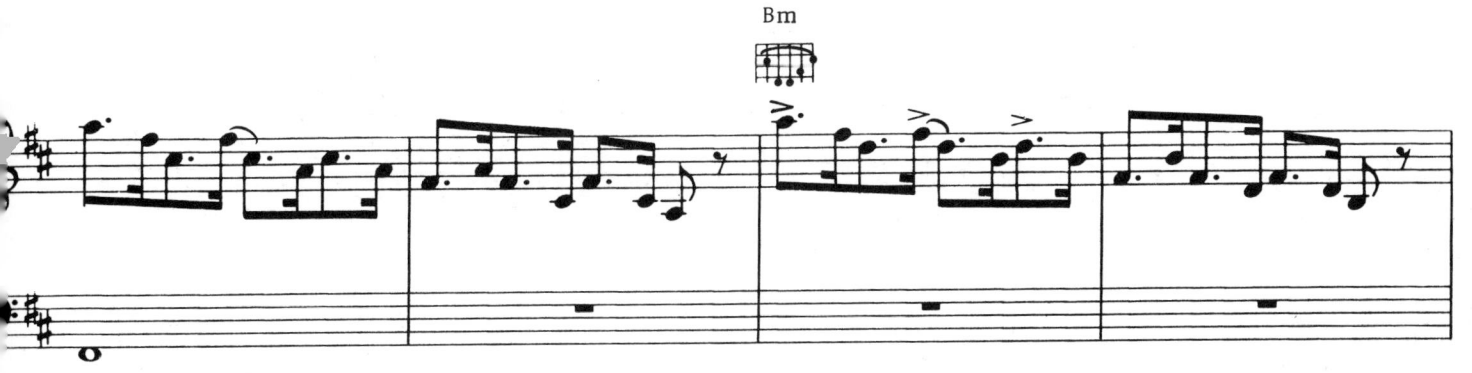

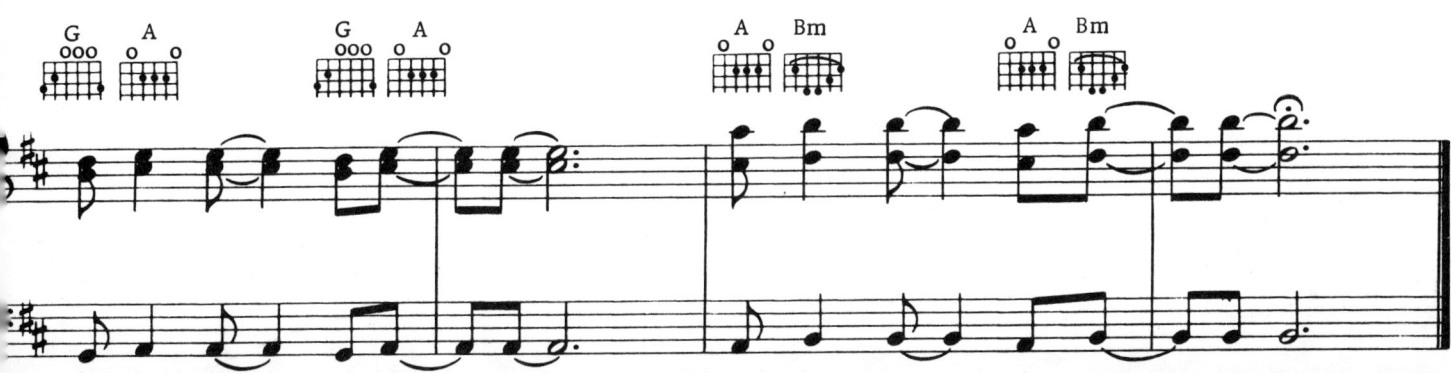

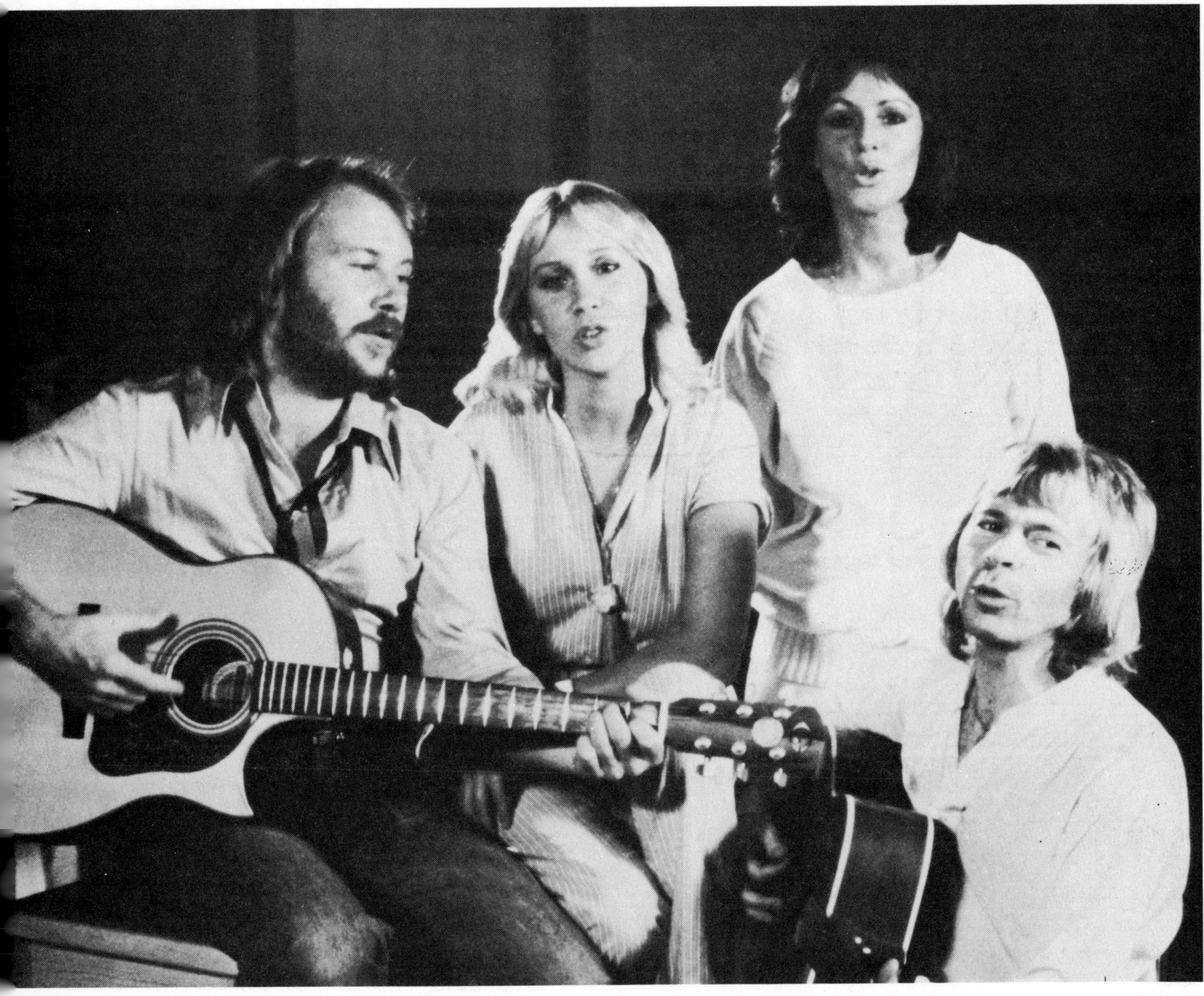

Man In The Middle

Words and Music by
Benny Andersson & Björn Ulvaeus

Did you see that man in the lim-ou-sine?
Did you see that man with the fat ci-gar?
Did you see that man made a big mis-take

With a pret-ty blonde; he is fif-ty and the
He just left his lunch with a bel-ly-full of
E-ven tho' he's got all his ser-vants and a

Copyright © 1975 Union Songs AB, Stockholm, Sweden for the world
Countless Songs Ltd. for U.S.A. and Canada
International Copyright Secured   All Rights Reserved

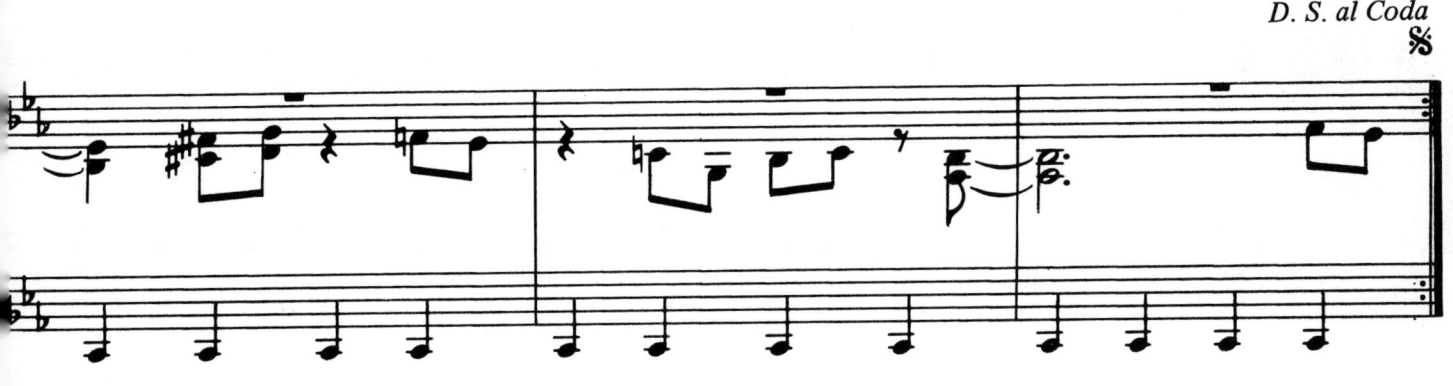

175

Money, Money, Money

Words and Music by
Benny Andersson & Björn Ulvaeus

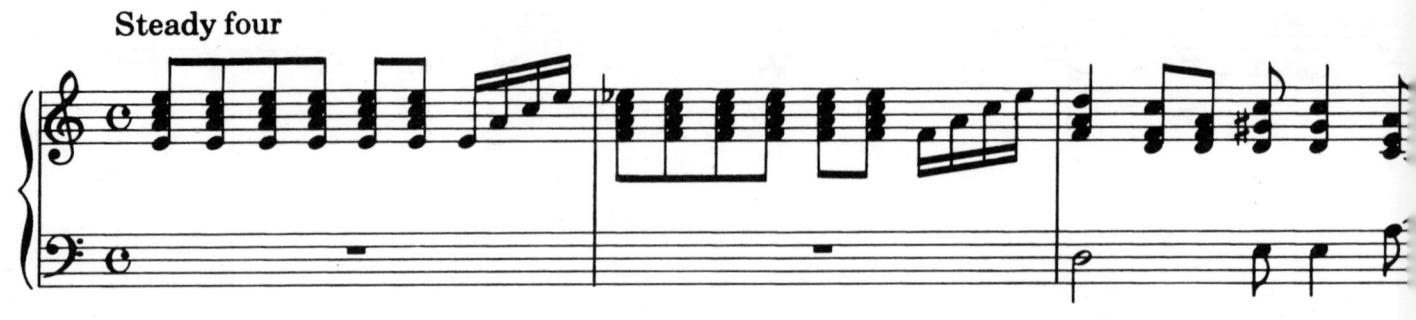

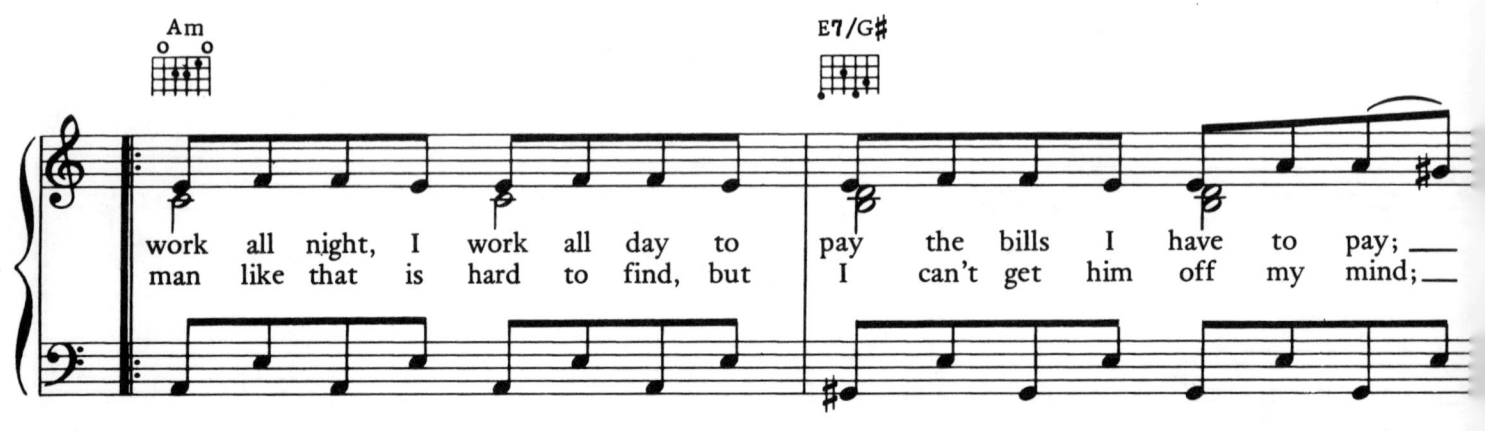

work all night, I work all day to pay the bills I have to pay; ___
man like that is hard to find, but I can't get him off my mind; ___

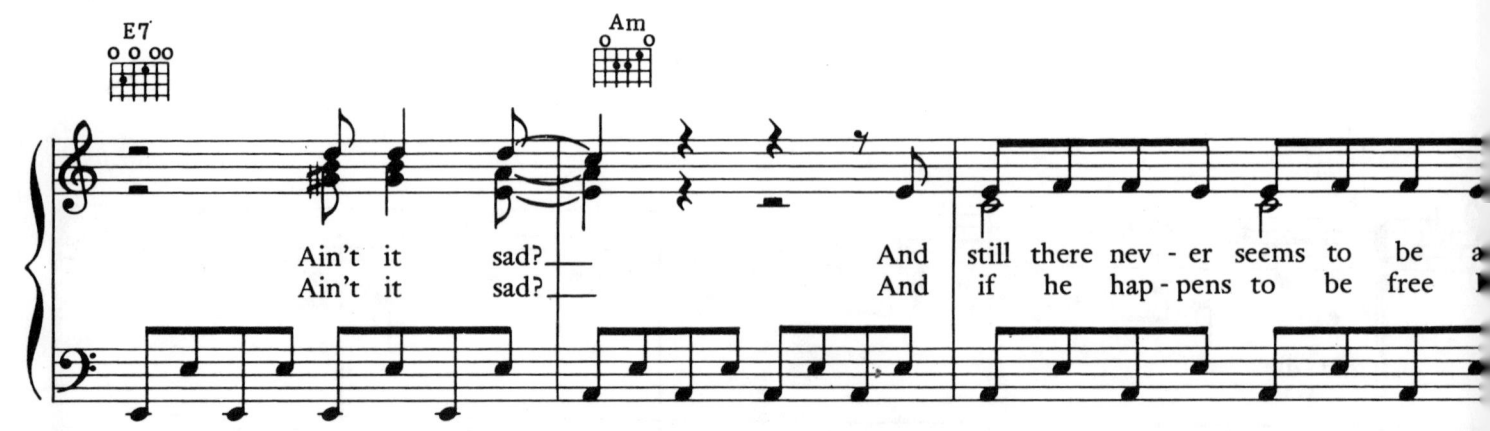

Ain't it sad? ___ And still there nev-er seems to be a
Ain't it sad? ___ And if he hap-pens to be free

Copyright © 1976 Union Songs AB, Stockholm, Sweden for the world
Artwork Music Co., Inc. for U.S.A. and Canada
International Copyright Secured   All Rights Reserved

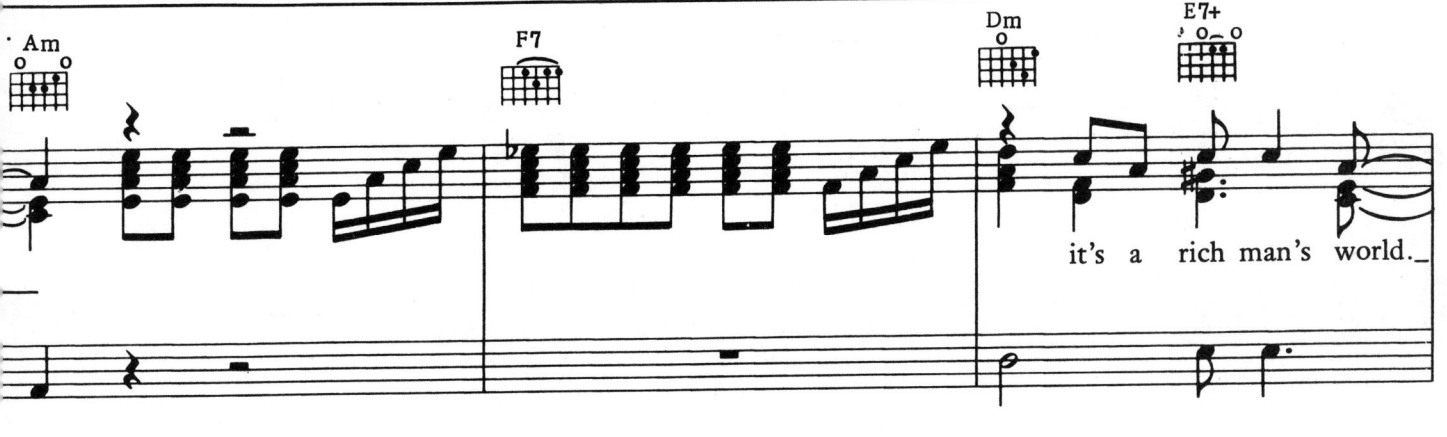

My Love, My Life

**Words and Music by
Benny Andersson, Björn Ulvaeus
and Stig Anderson**

I've seen it on your face, tells me more than any
I've watched you look away,

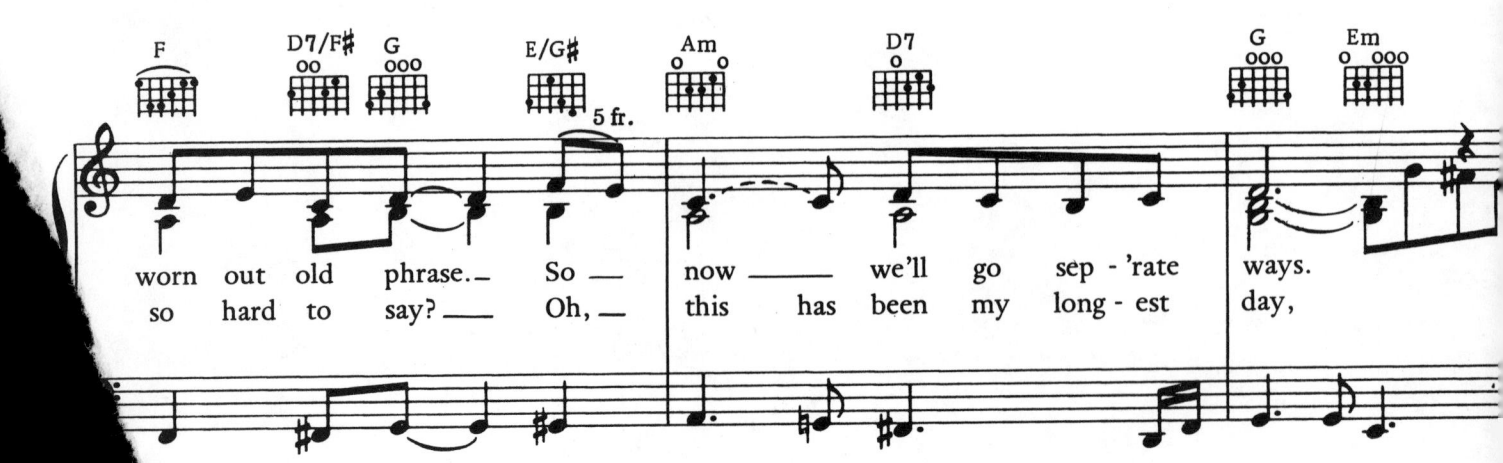

worn out old phrase. So now we'll go sep-'rate ways.
so hard to say? Oh, this has been my long-est day,

Copyright © 1976 Polar Music AB, Stockholm, Sweden for the world
Artwork Music Co., Inc. for U.S.A. and Canada
International Copyright Secured   All Rights Reserved

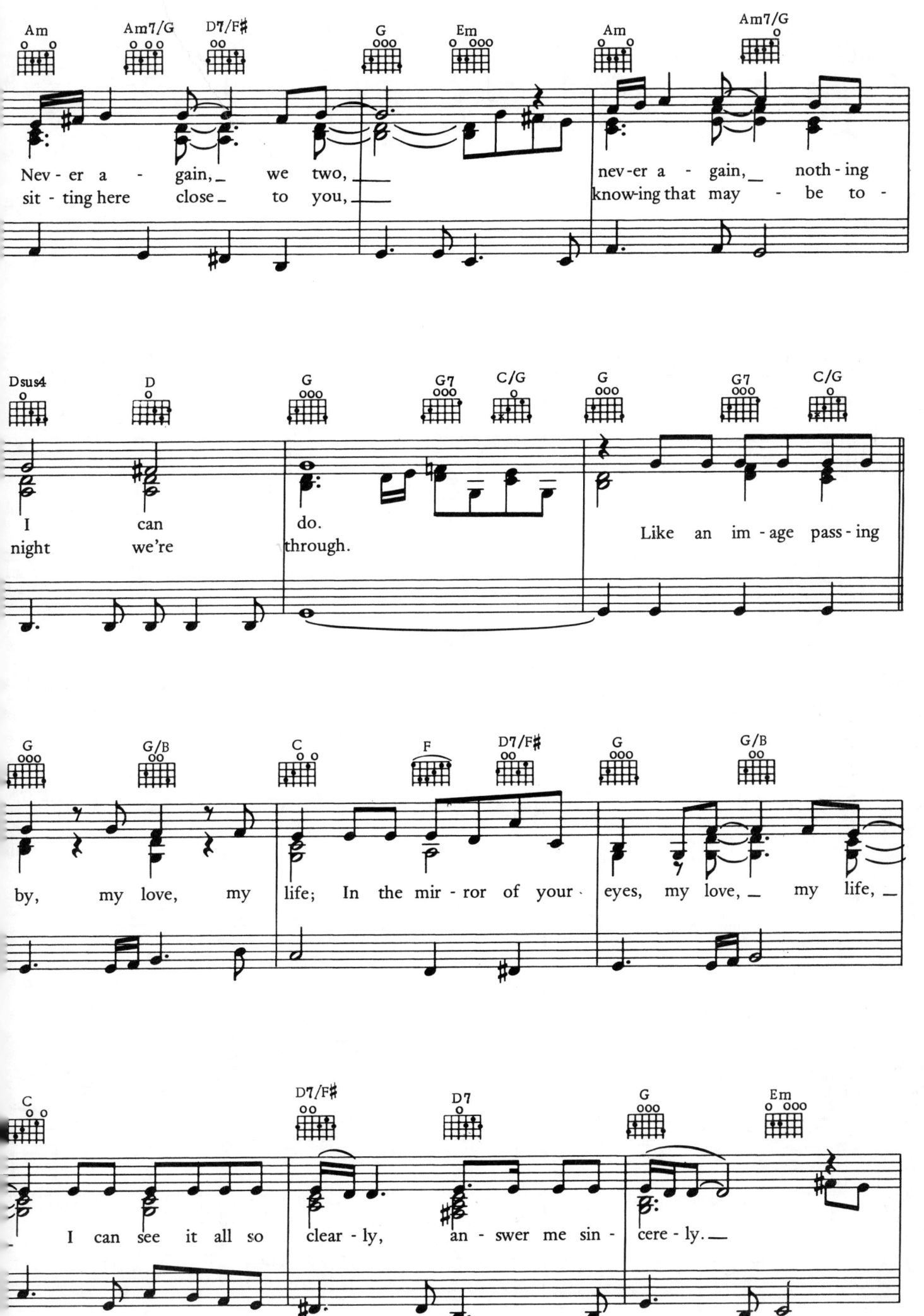

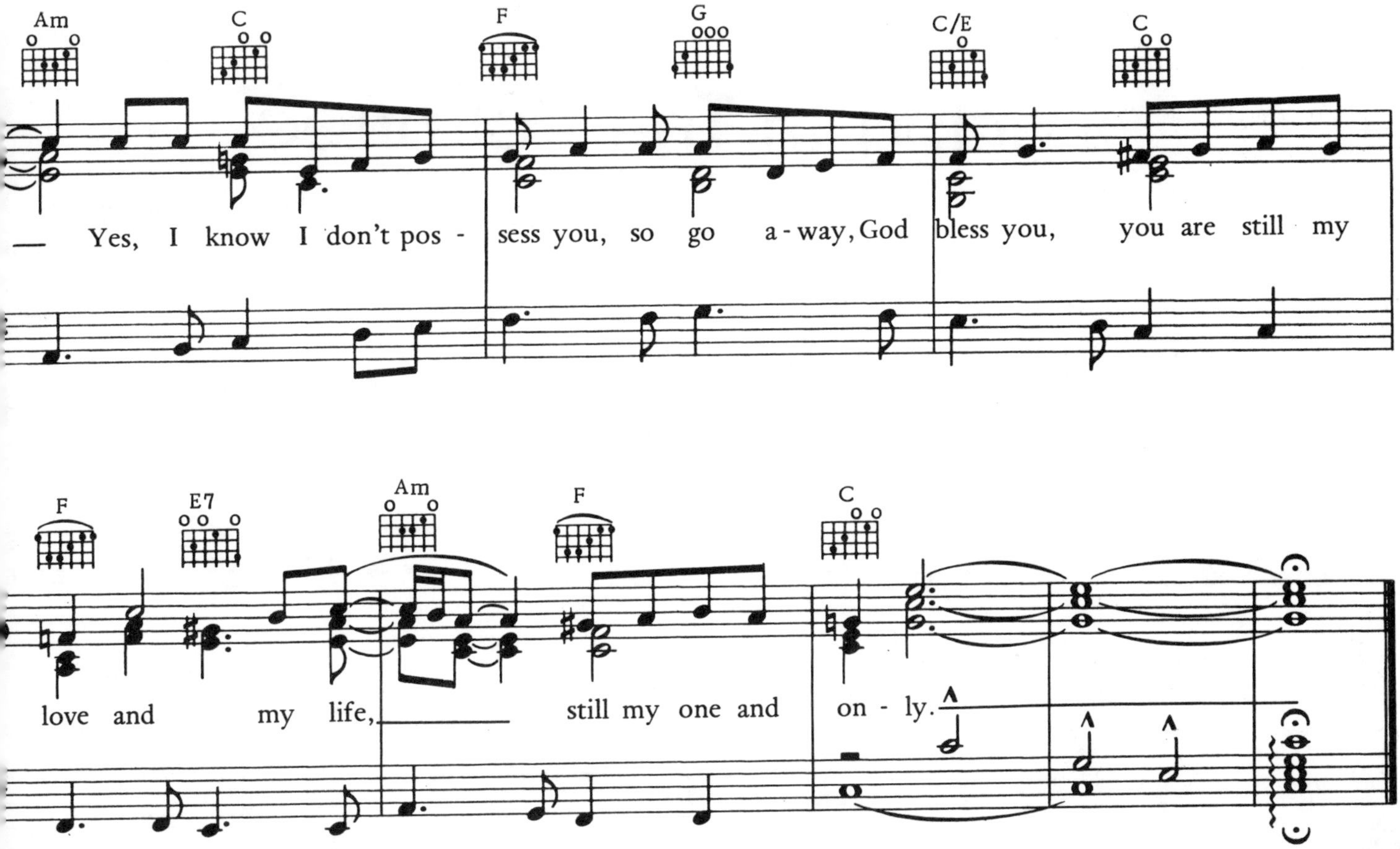
Am C F G C/E C
— Yes, I know I don't pos - sess you, so go a - way, God bless you, you are still my
F E7 Am F C
love and my life, still my one and on - ly.

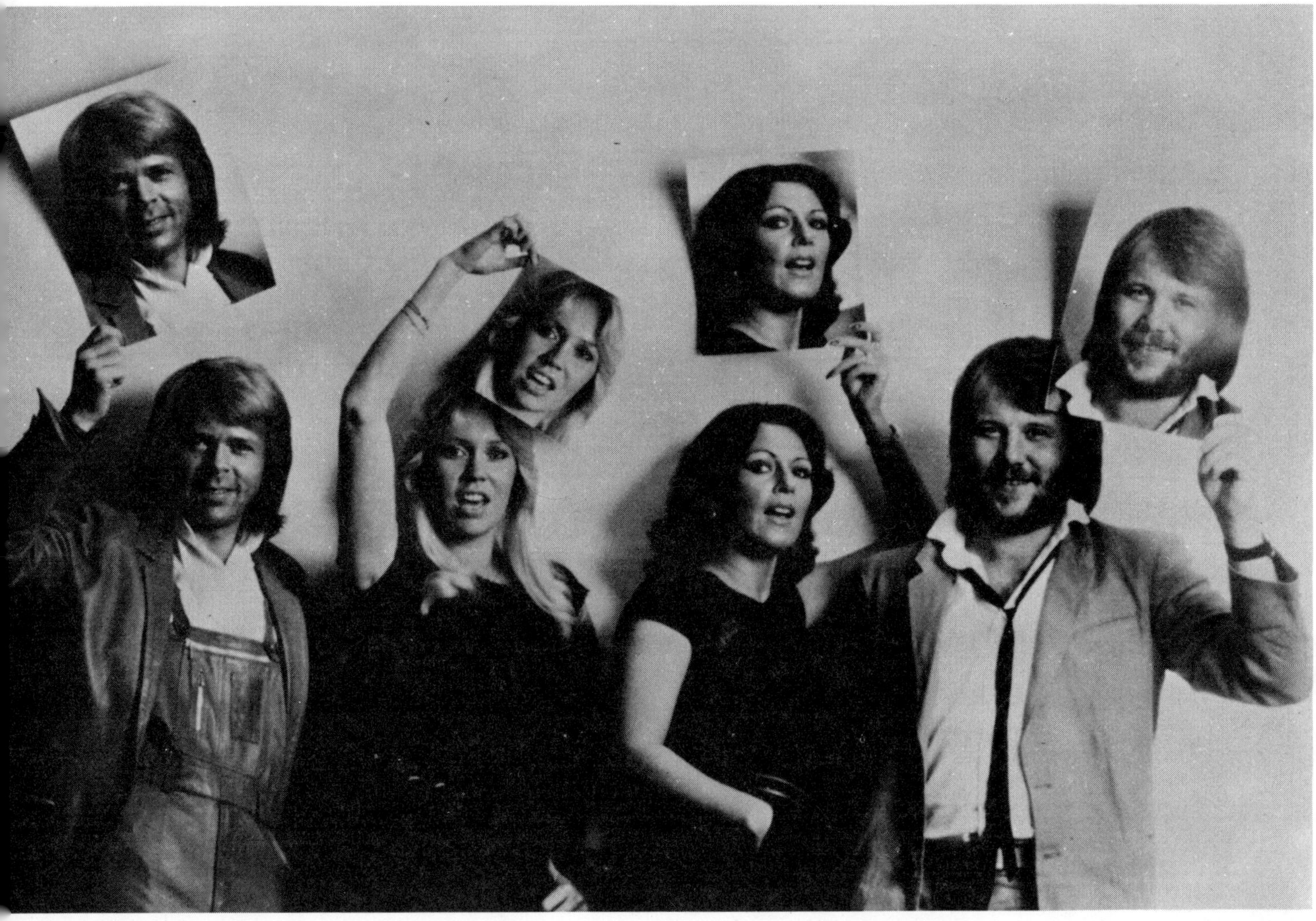

Sitting In The Palmtree

Words and Music by
Benny Andersson & Björn Ulvaeus

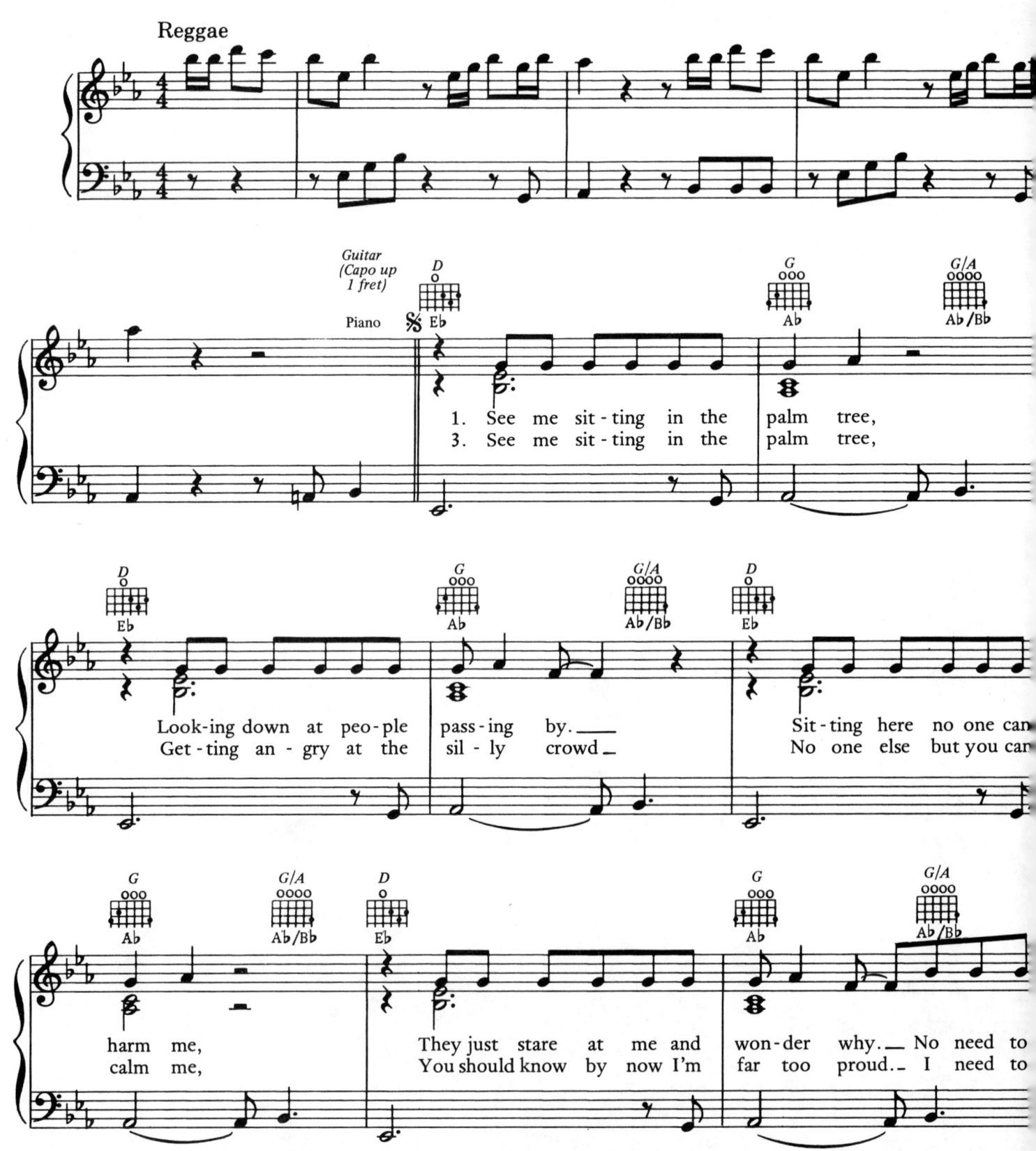

186

Move On

G/B Am7 Em C
Bb/D Cm7 Gm Eb
D. S. al C
G/B Am D G Gsus4 G Gsus4
Bb/D Cm F Bb Bbsus4 Bb Bbsus4
tr
Coda
C G
Eb Bb
on.
Like a wind that's al-w
D Am Em G
F Cm Gm Bb
blow - ing, life is flow - ing, move on.
Like the sun-rise in th

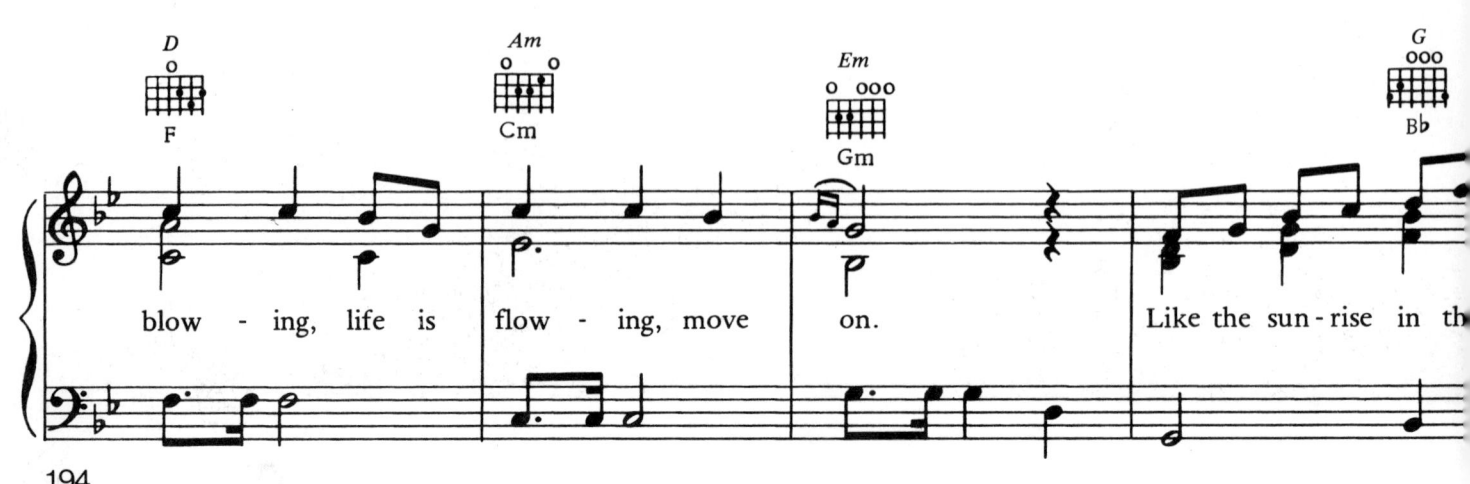

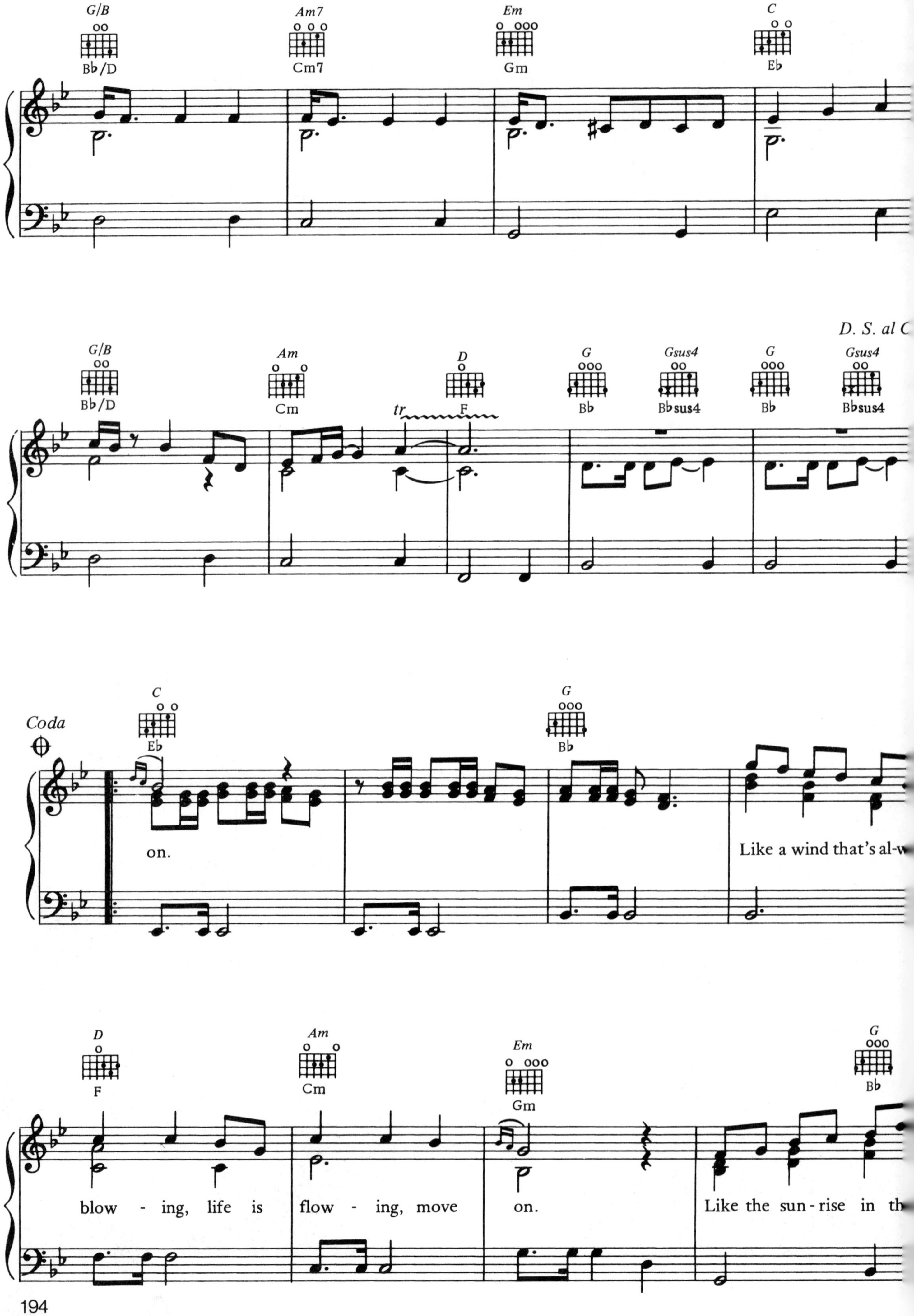

C
E♭
G
B♭
morn - ing, life is dawn - ing, move on. How I treas - ure ev - 'ry
D
F
Am
Cm
D
F
Repeat and fade
min - ute be - ing part of be - ing in it with the urge to move

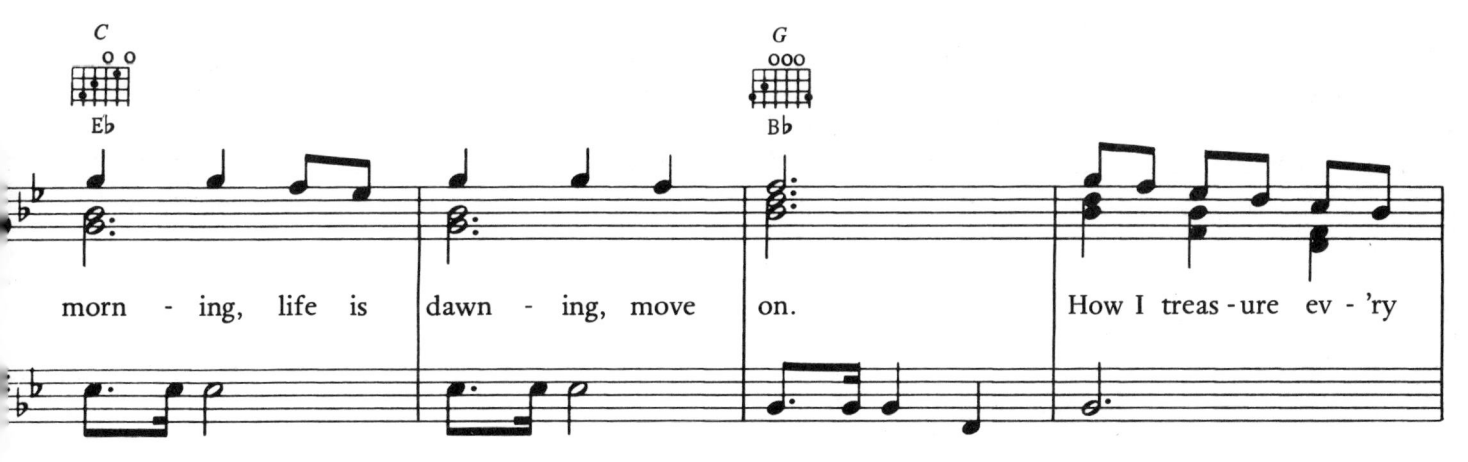

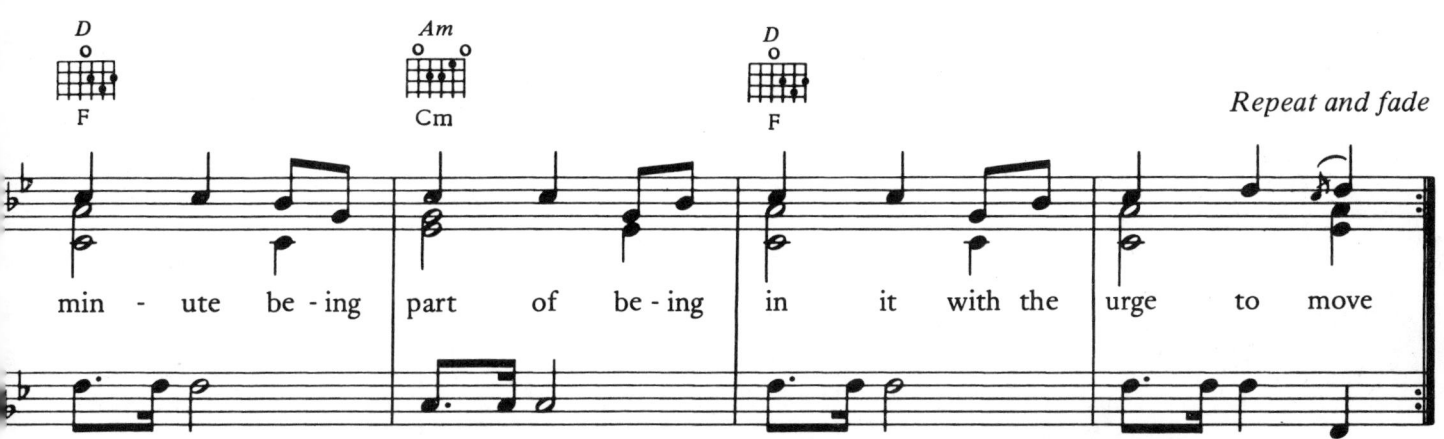

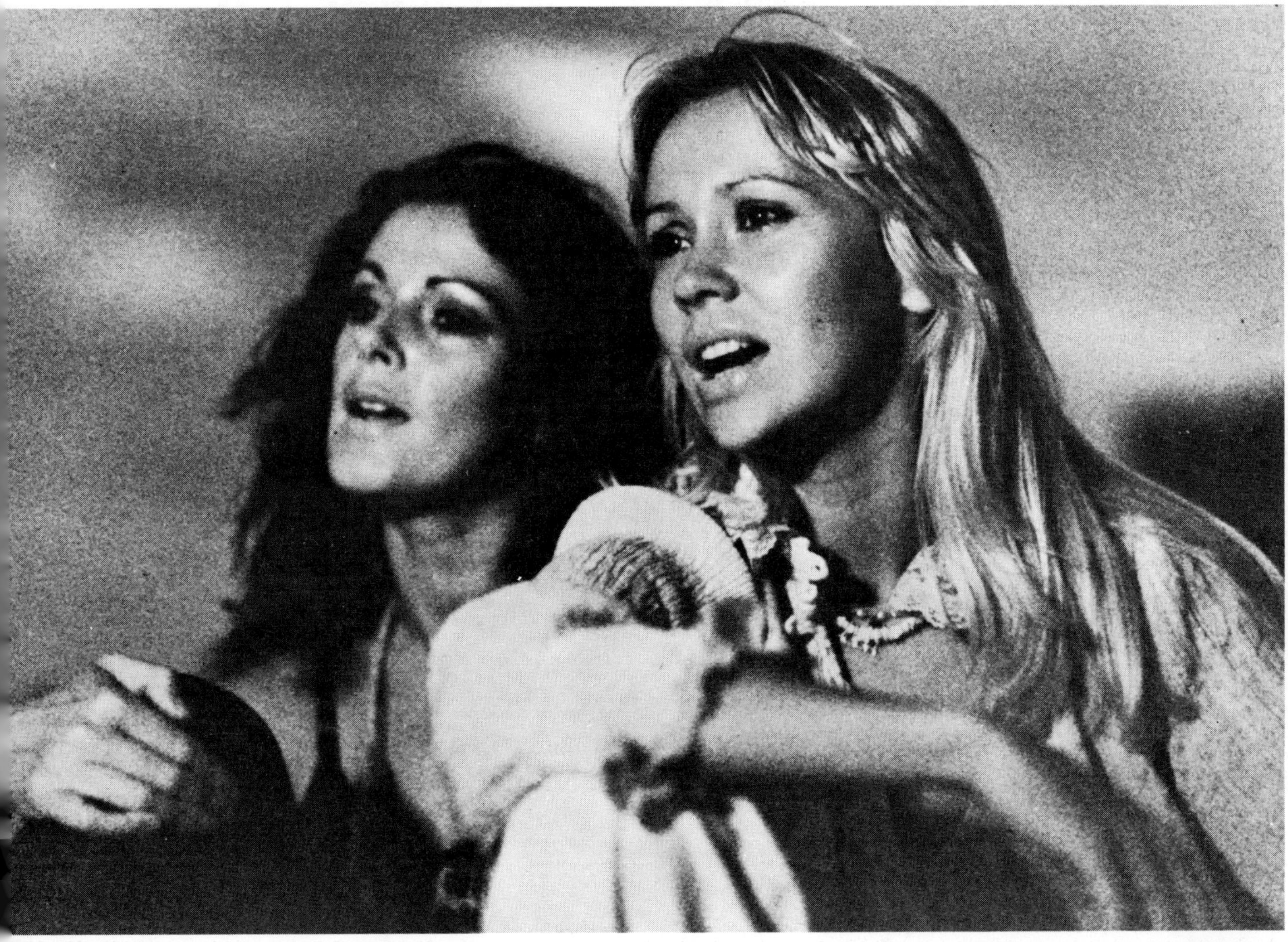

F A7 Dm Dm/C
A C#7 F#m F#m/E
says I be - gan to sing long be - fore I could talk.
G7 G+ C G/B
B7 B+ E B/D#
And I've of - ten won - dered how did it all start? Who
C C+ F Fm Am
E E+ A Am C#m
found out that noth - ing can cap - ture a heart like a mel - o - dy can?
F Dm Dm/C G7
A F#m F#m7/E B7
Well, who - ev - er it was, I'm a fan. So I say,

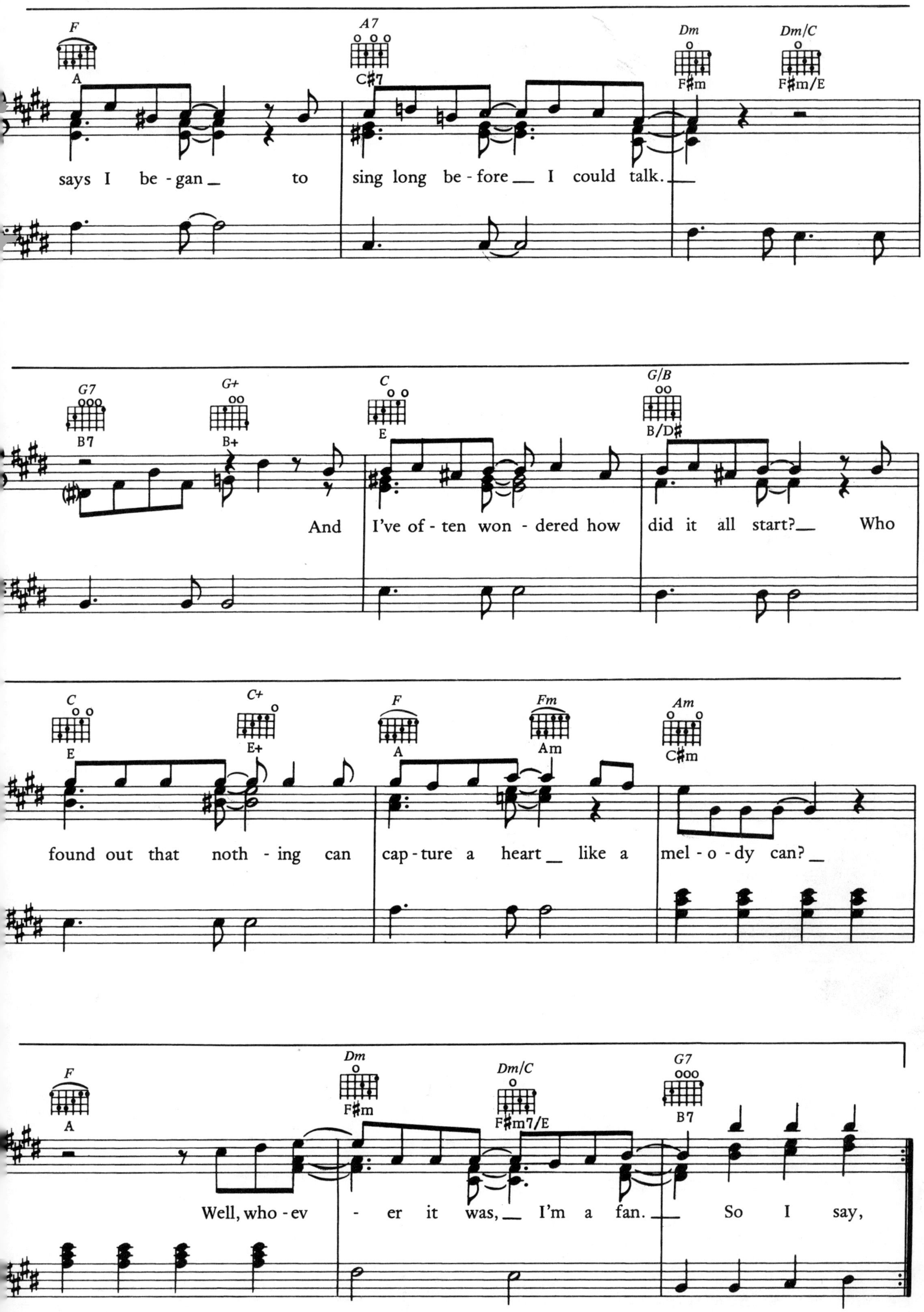

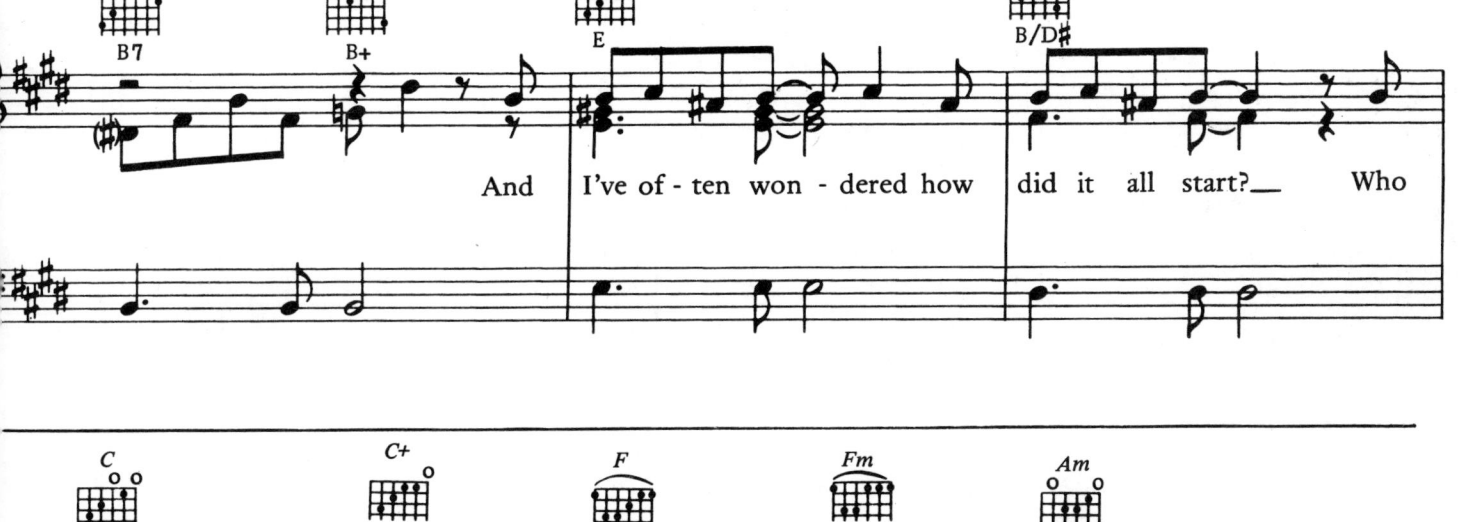

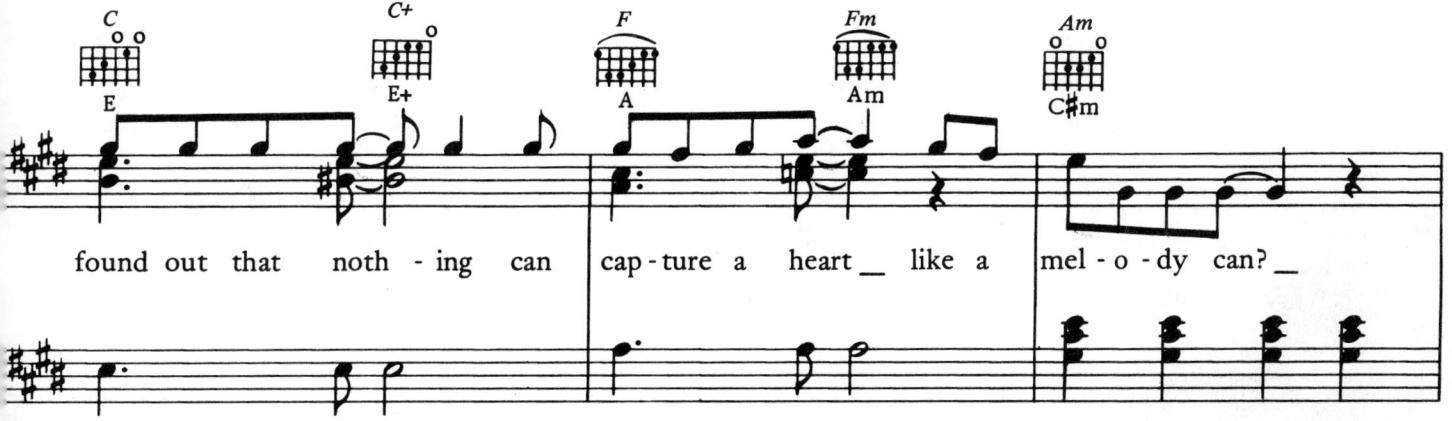

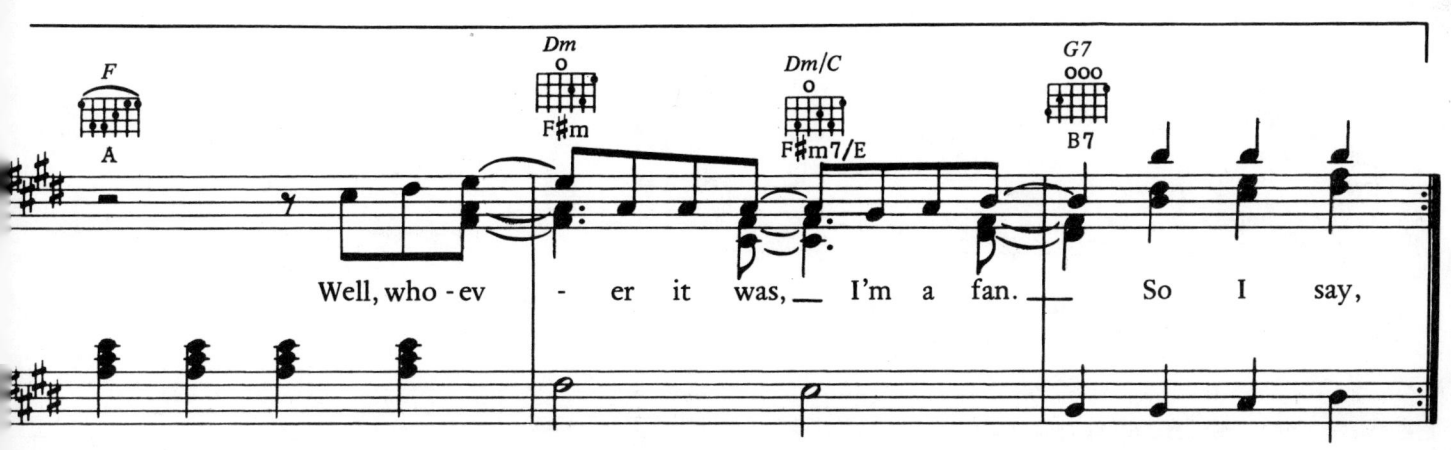

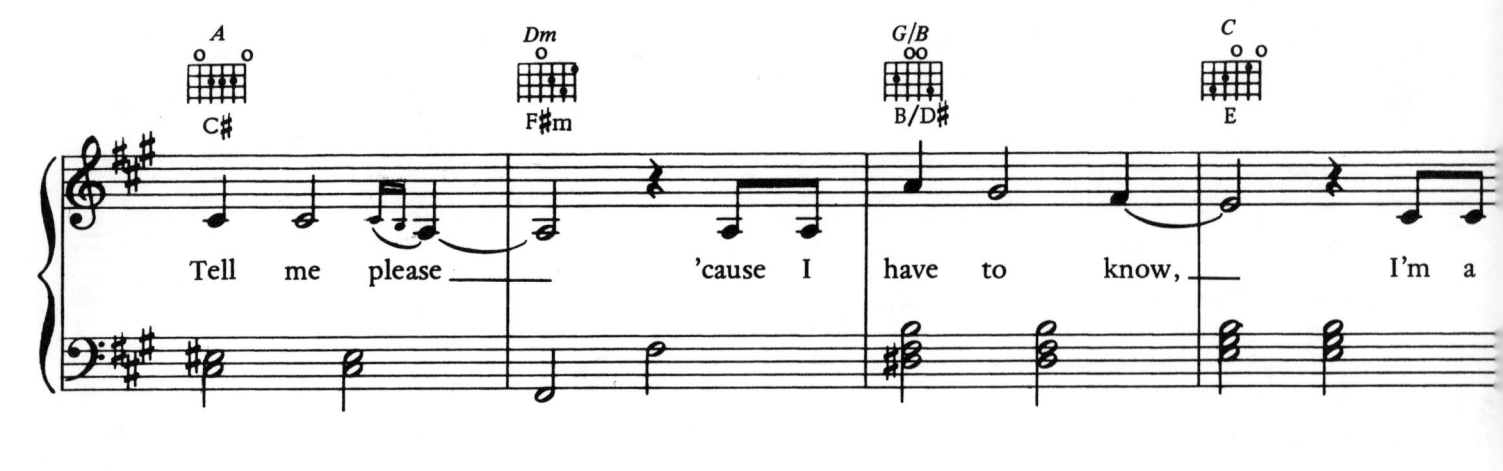

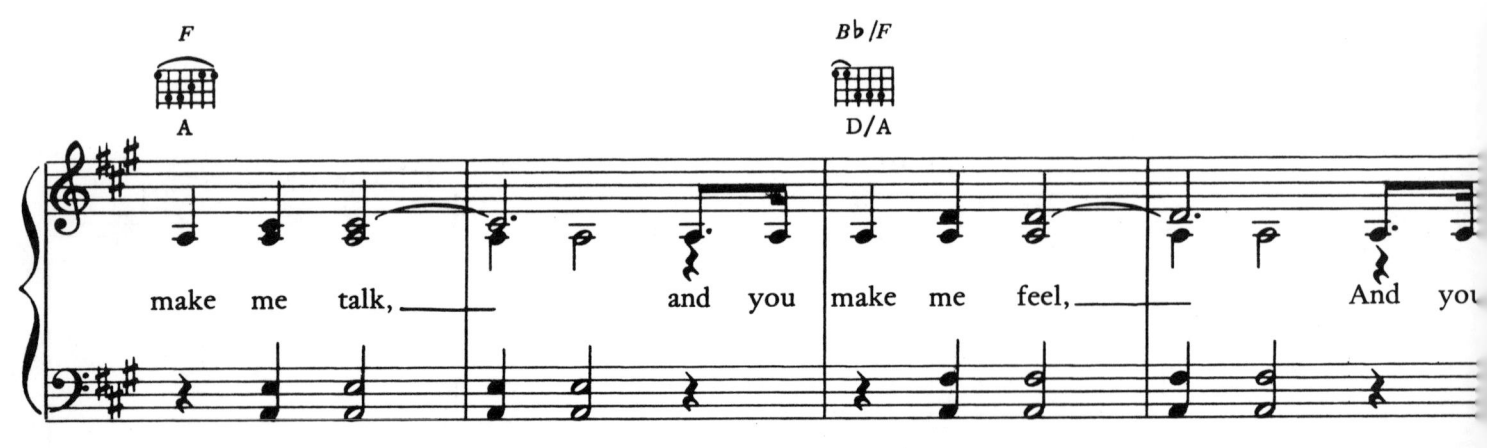

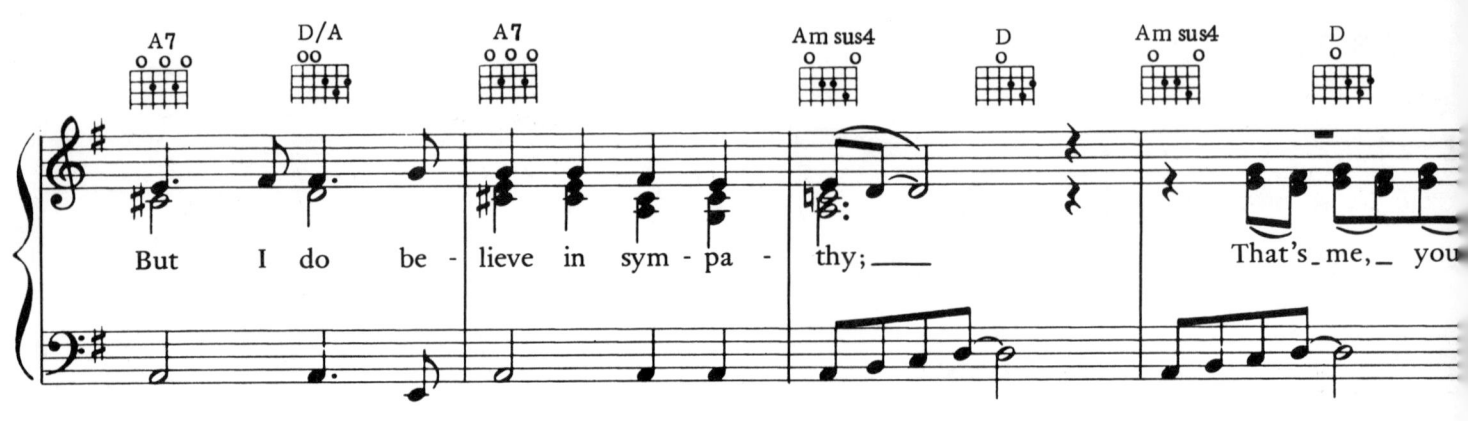
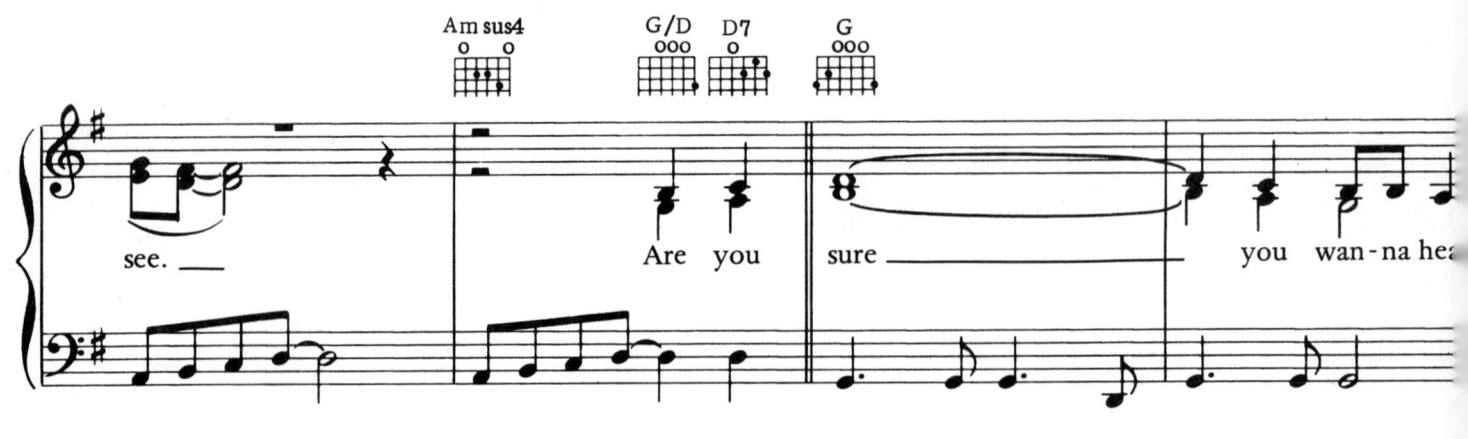

210

My Mama Said

Words and Music by
Benny Andersson & Björn Ulvaeus

Moderate Rock

Tried to sneak out with-out say-ing
In the morn-ing she said, "Lis-ten."
With my loud-est rec-ord
Oh, I felt like in a

play-ing. Oh oh my ma-ma said,
pris-on. Yeah-eah my ma-ma said,
"Look at this, you have-n't done your
"I know you've been out a-gain with

Copyright © 1973 Union Songs AB, Stockholm, Sweden for the world
Countless Songs Ltd. for U.S.A. and Canada
International Copyright Secured   All Rights Reserved

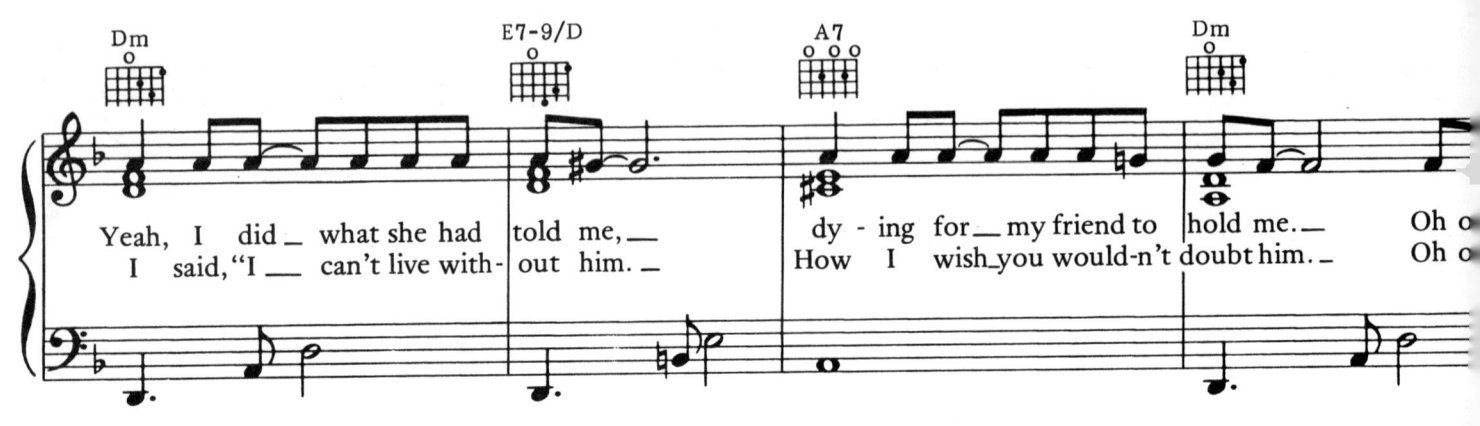

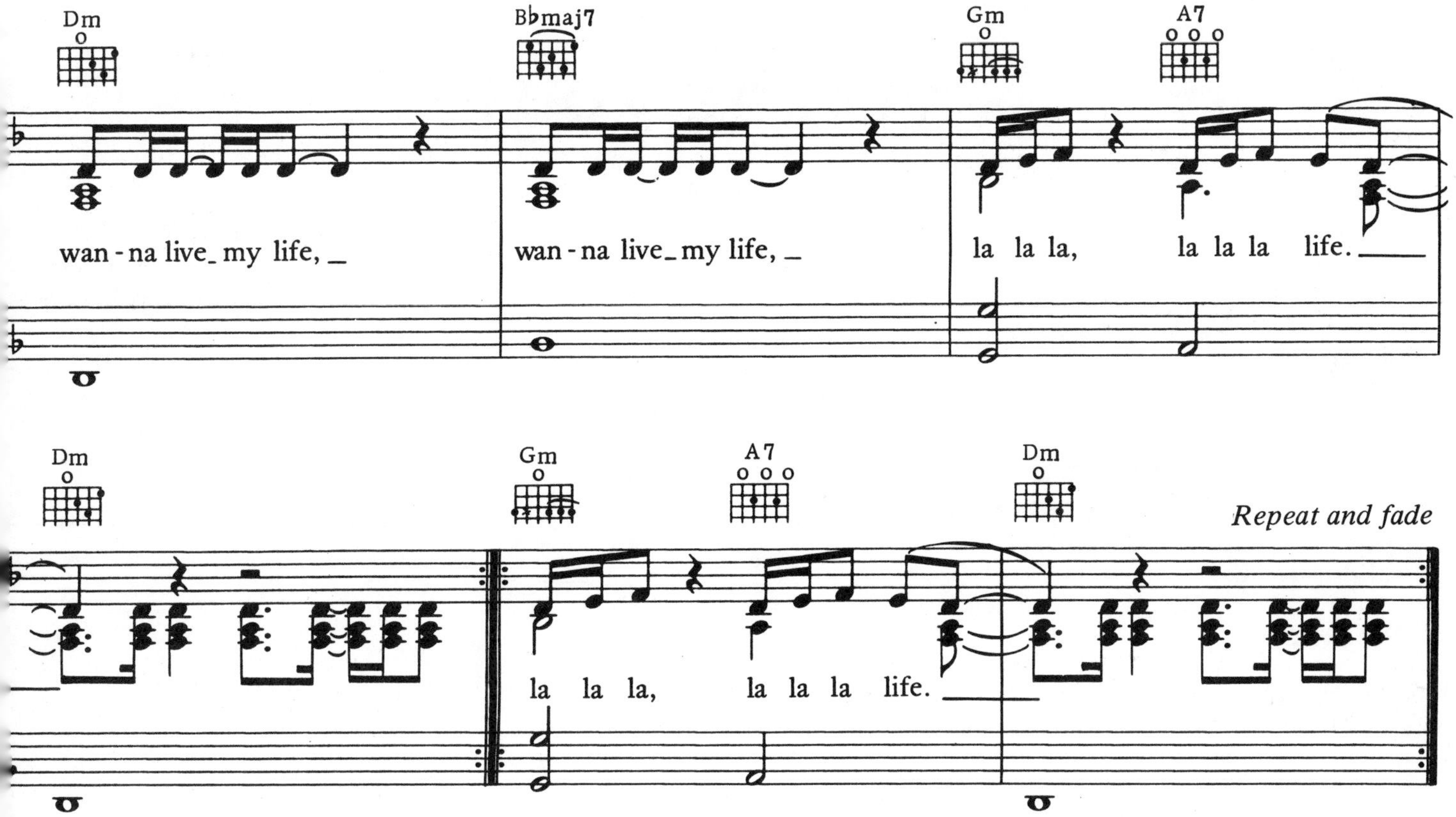
Dm
Bbmaj7
Gm
A7
wan - na live_ my life, _
wan - na live_ my life, _
la la la, la la la life. ____
Dm
Gm
A7
Dm
Repeat and fade
la la la, la la la life. ____

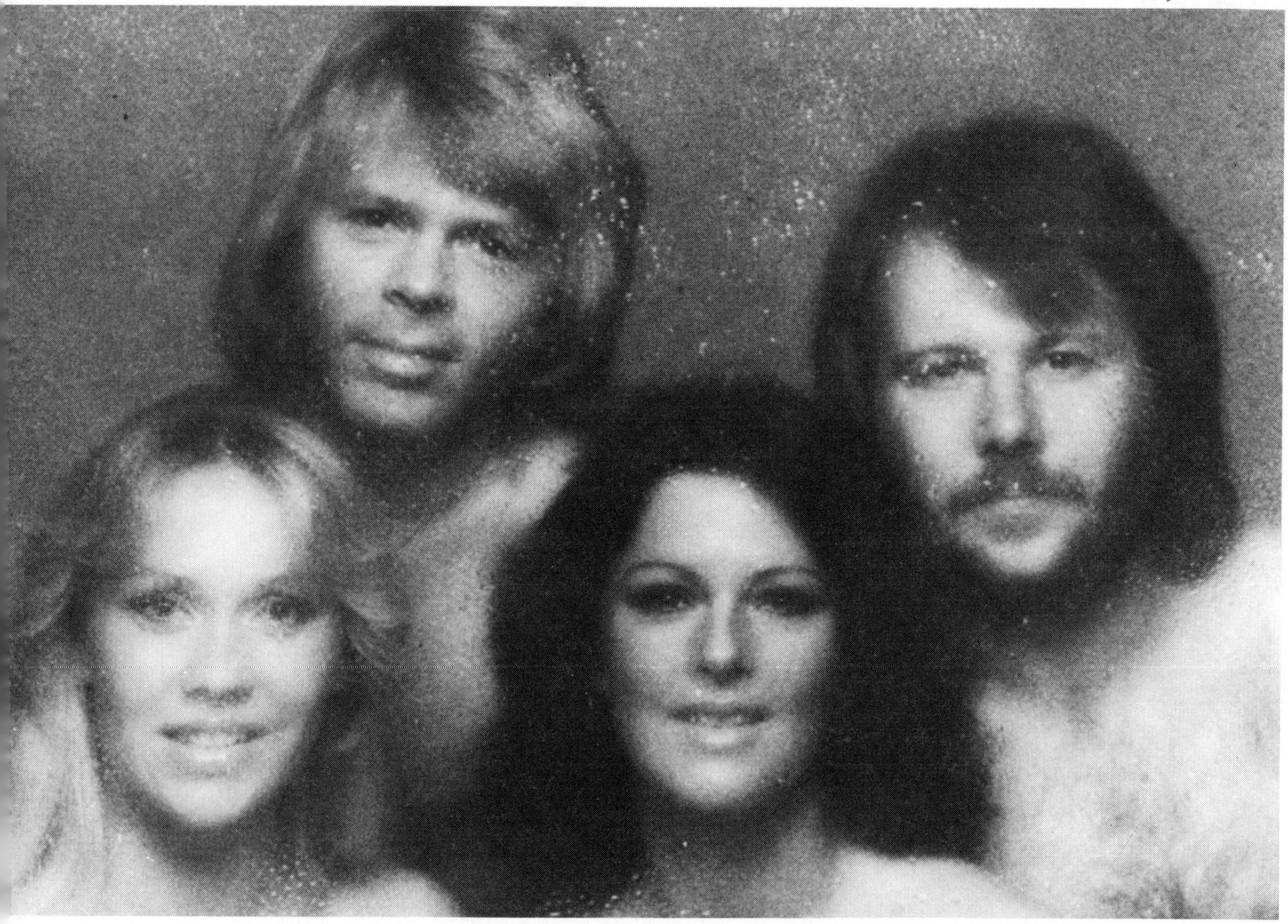

Voulez-Vous

Words and Music by
Benny Andersson & Björn Ulvaeus

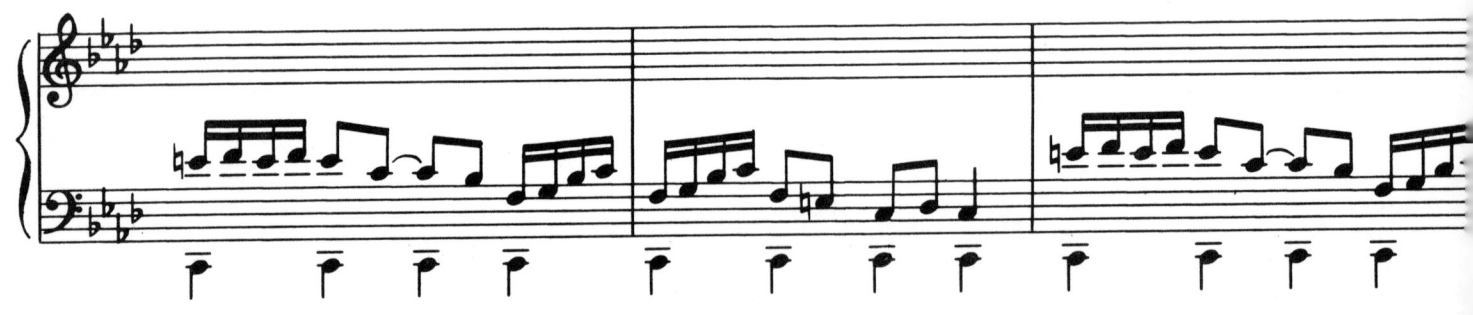
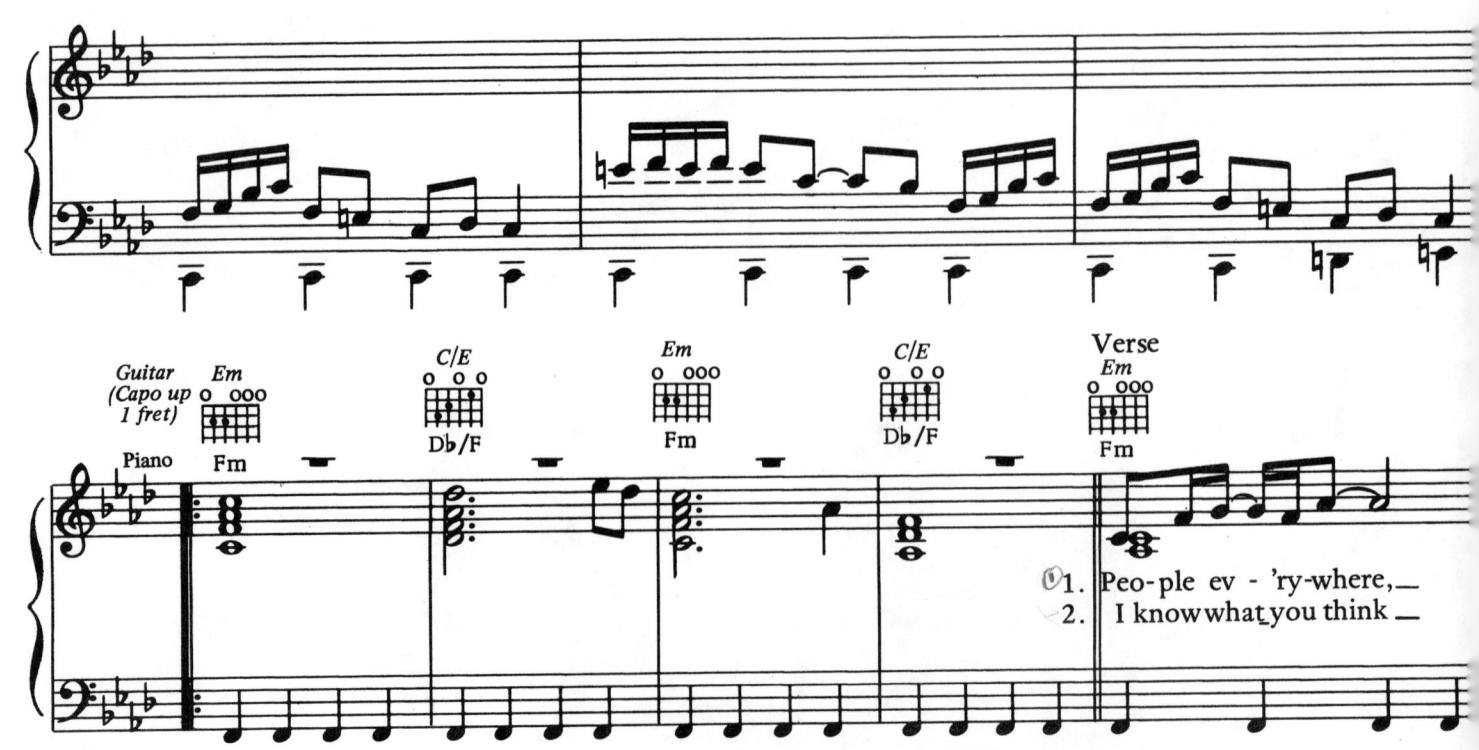

Copyright © 1979 Union Songs AB, Stockholm, Sweden for the world
Artwork Music Co., Inc. for U.S.A. and Canada
International Copyright Secured   All Rights Reserved

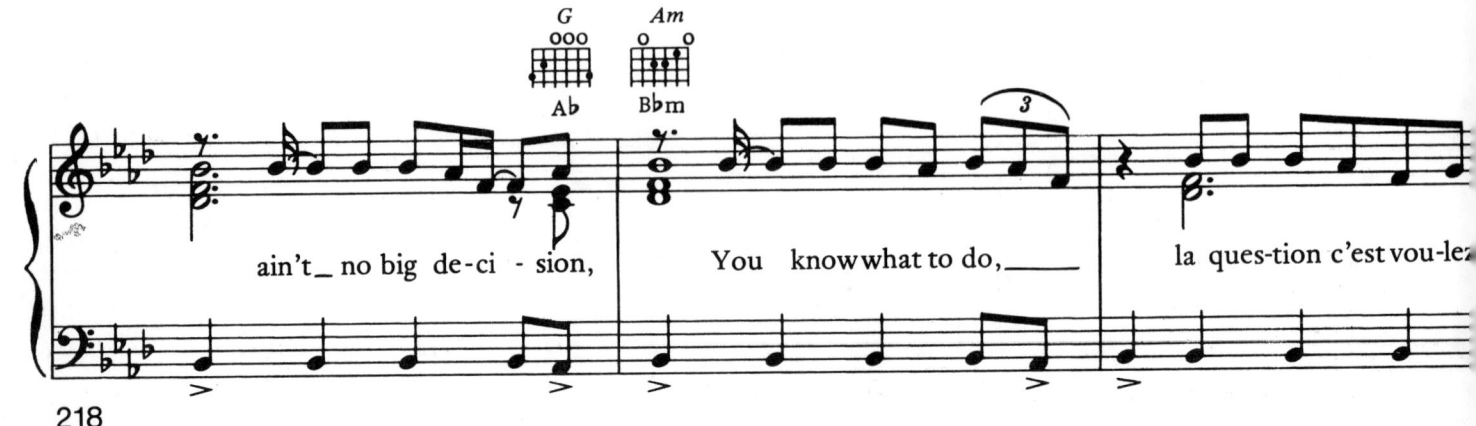

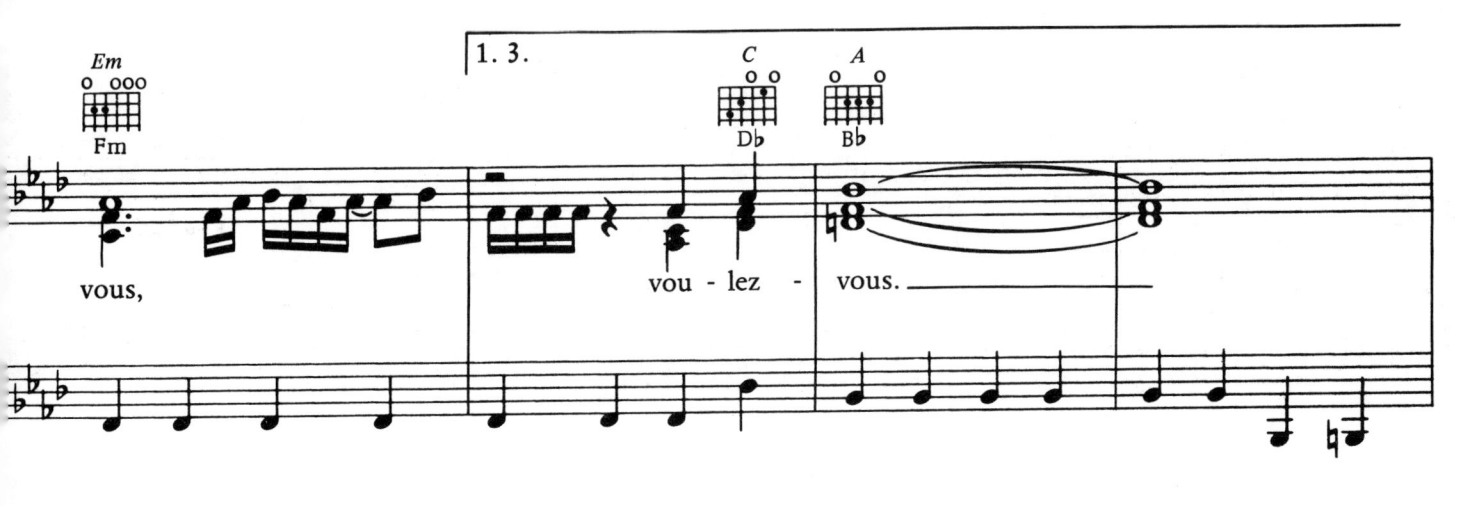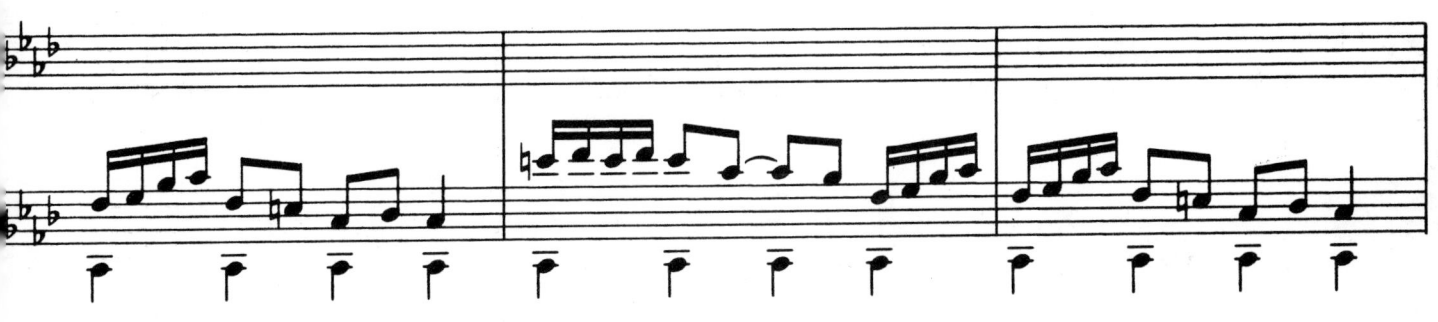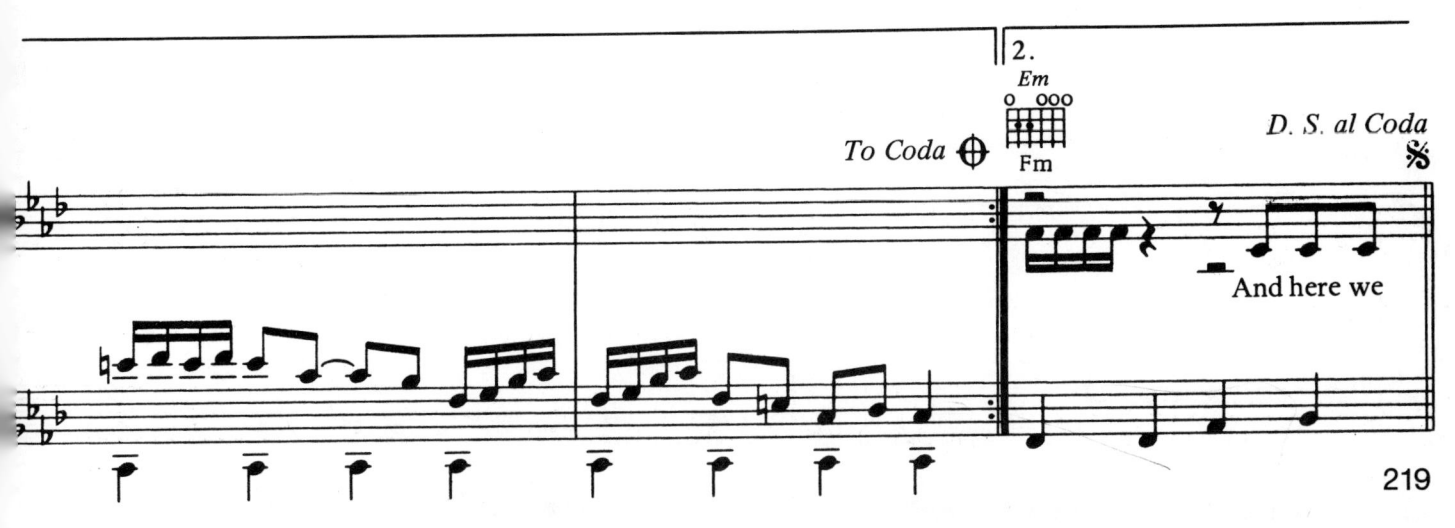

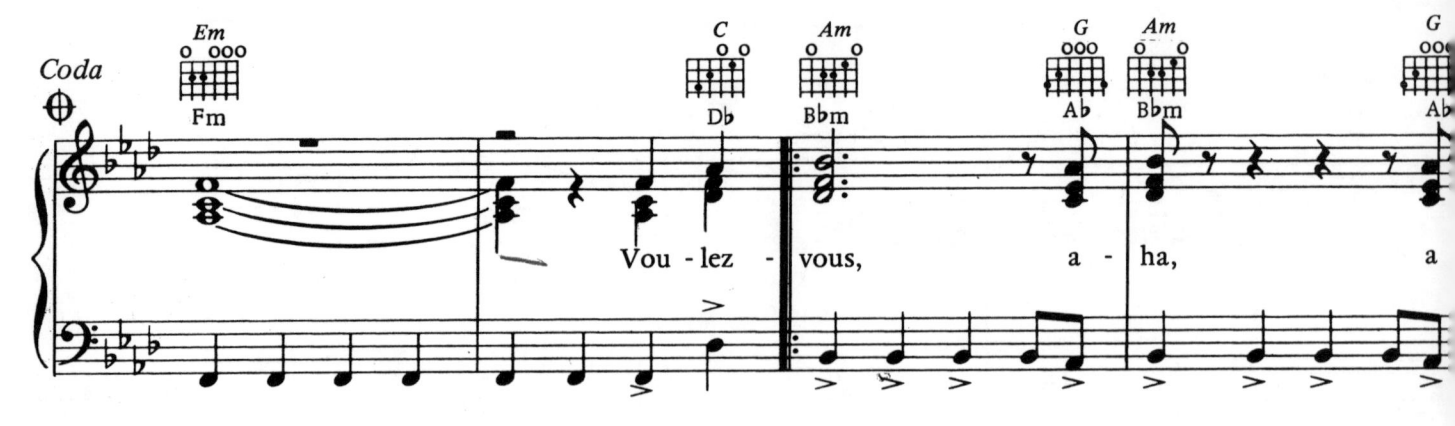
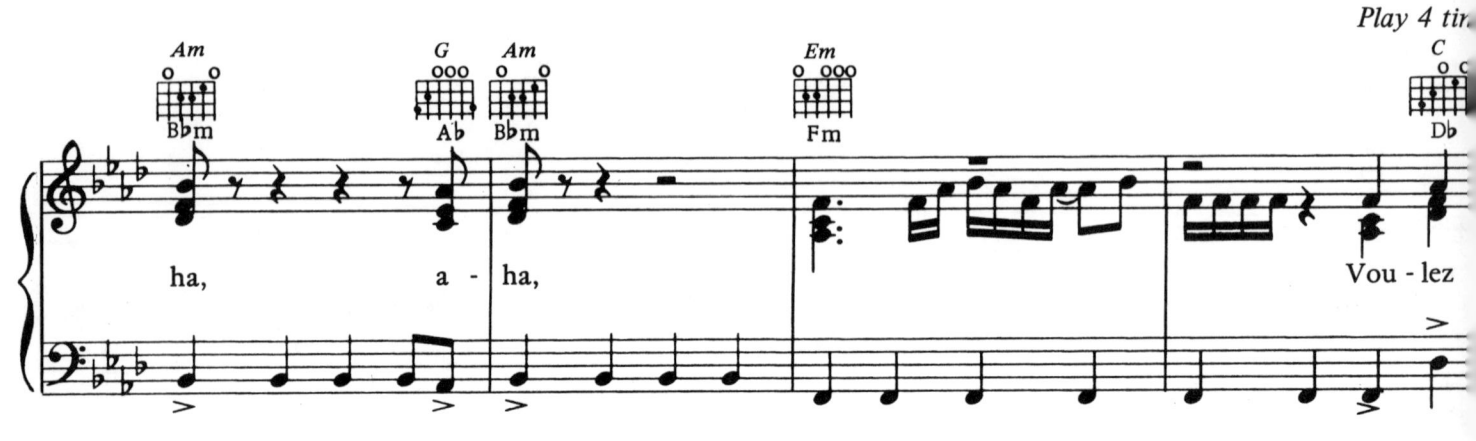

Nina, Pretty Ballerina

Words and Music by
Benny Andersson & Björn Ulvaeus

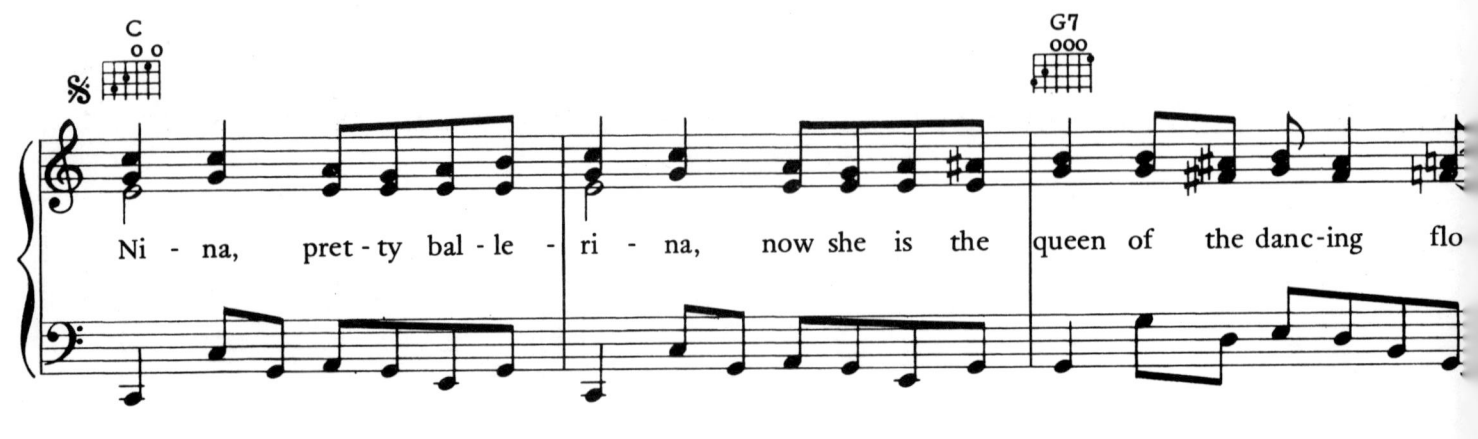

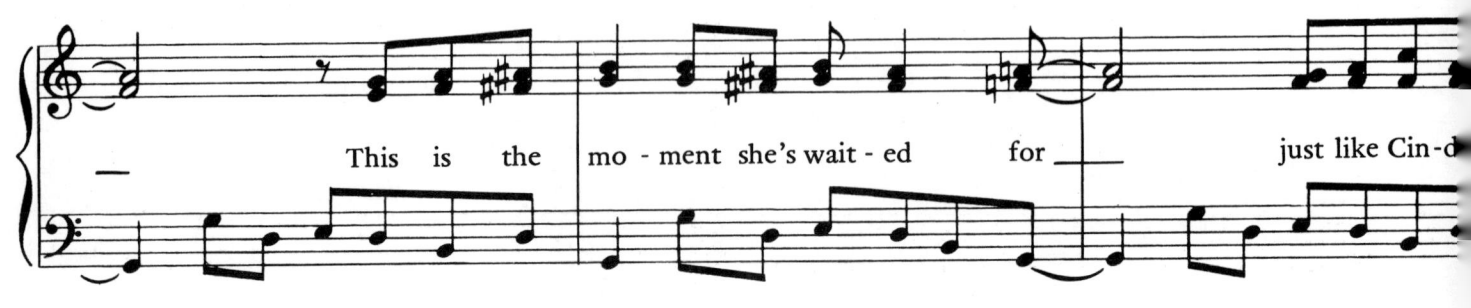

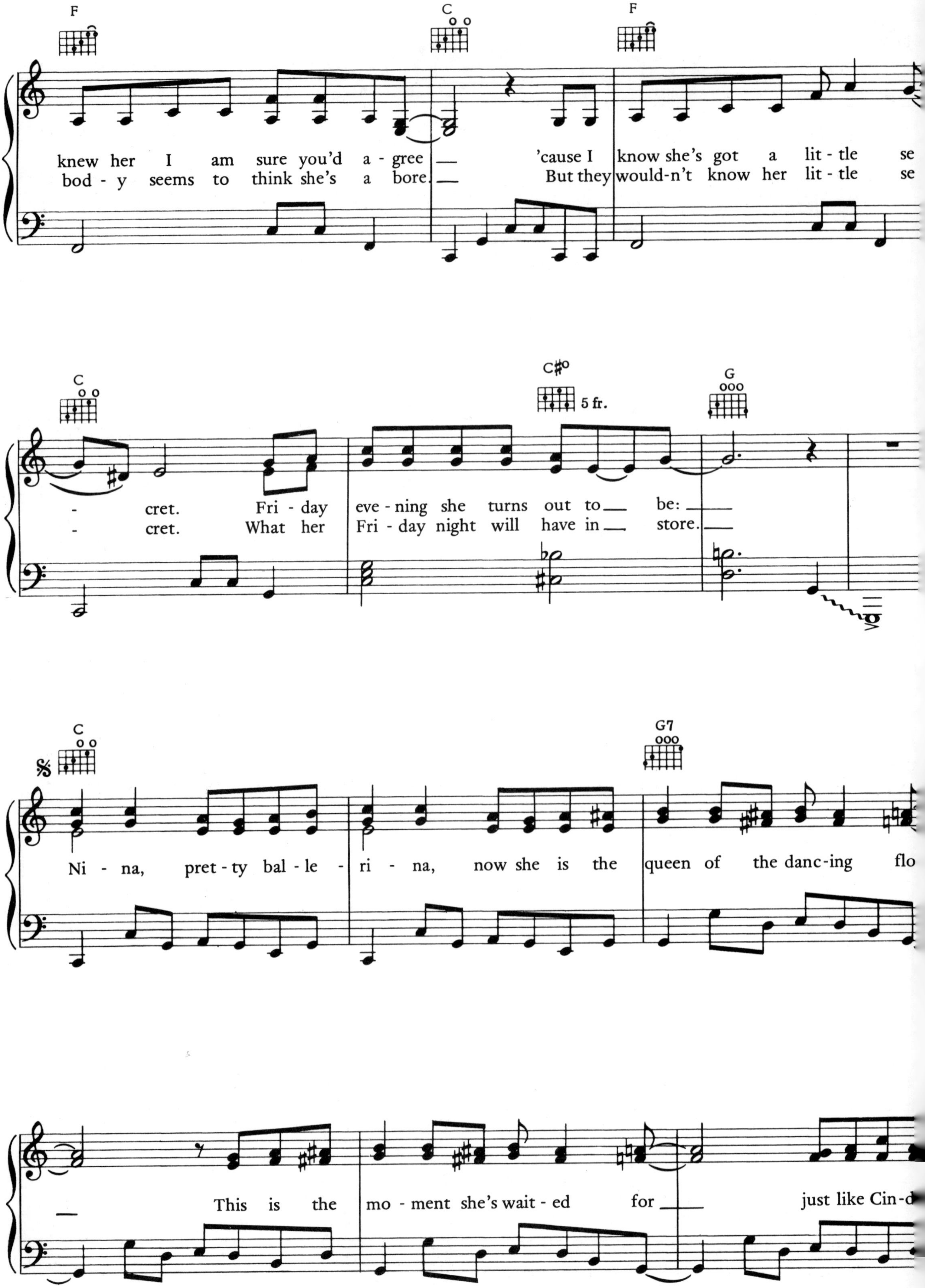
F
C
F
knew her I am sure you'd a - gree — 'cause I know she's got a lit - tle se
bod - y seems to think she's a bore. — But they would-n't know her lit - tle se
C
C#o
5 fr.
G
- cret. Fri - day eve - ning she turns out to — be: —
- cret. What her Fri - day night will have in — store. —
C
G7
Ni - na, pret - ty bal - le - ri - na, now she is the queen of the danc - ing flo
— This is the mo - ment she's wait - ed for — just like Cin - d

People Need Love

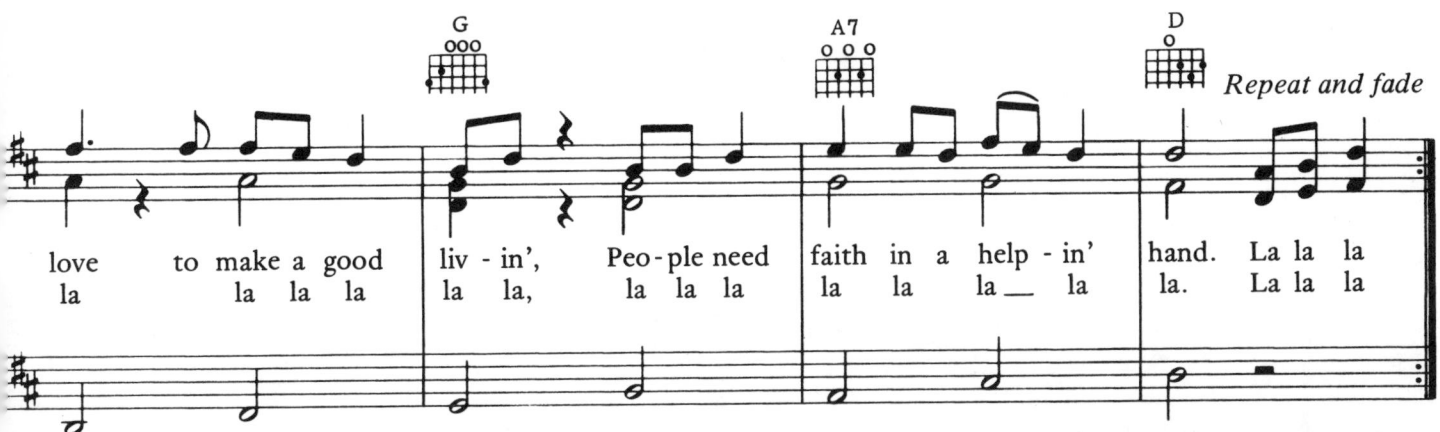

photo: HANSER/POLAR MUSIC INT'L AB

Rock Me

Words and Music by
Benny Andersson & Björn Ulvaeus

Copyright © 1976 Union Songs AB, Stockholm, Sweden for the world
Countless Songs Ltd. for U.S.A. and Canada
International Copyright Secured   All Rights Reserved

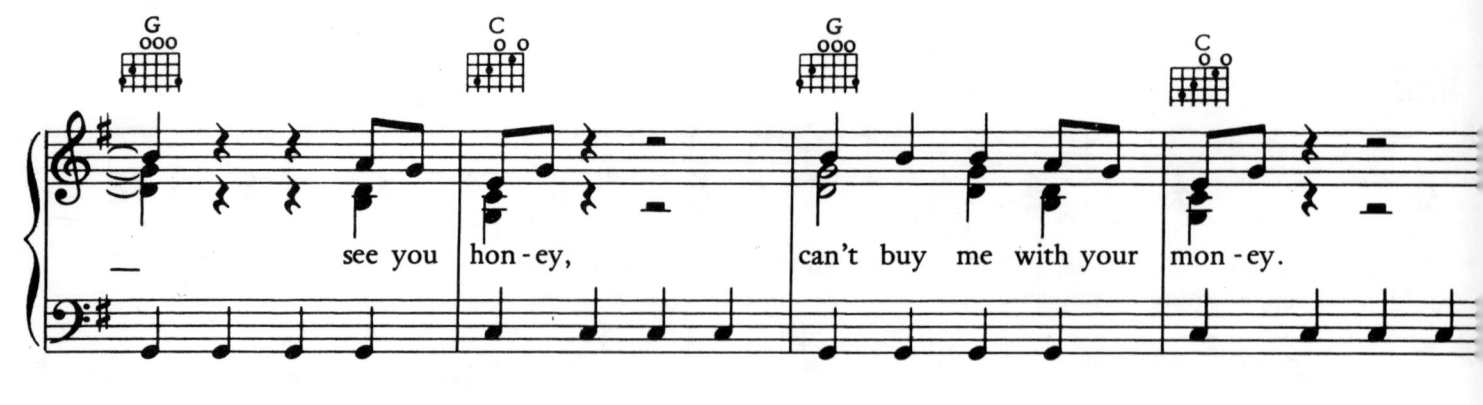

SOS

Words and Music by
Benny Andersson, Björn Ulvaeus
and Stig Anderson

Where are those hap-py days, they seem so hard to find?
You seem so far a-way though you are stand-ing near.

Copyright © 1975 Union Songs AB, Stockholm, Sweden for the world
Countless Songs Ltd. for U.S.A. and Canada
International Copyright Secured   All Rights Reserved

E B F♯m A E A/E E
F C Gm B♭ F B♭/F F
So when you're near me, dar - ling, can't you hear me S. O. S.
A/E E B F♯m A
B♭/F F C Gm B♭
The love you gave me, noth - ing else can save me, S.
E A/E E A
F B♭/F F B♭
O. S.
When you're gone how can I
C D E
D♭ E♭ F
even try to go on?
When you're gone

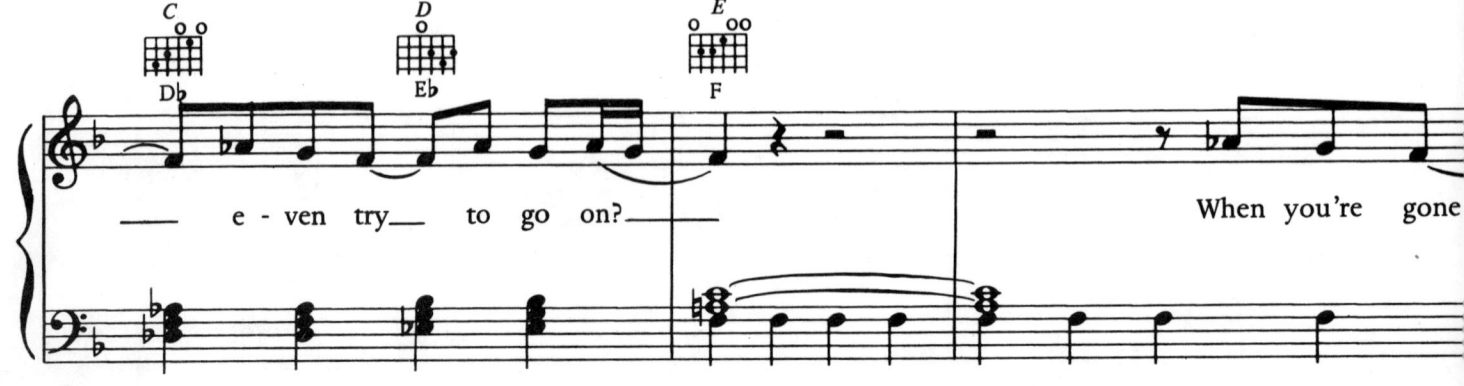

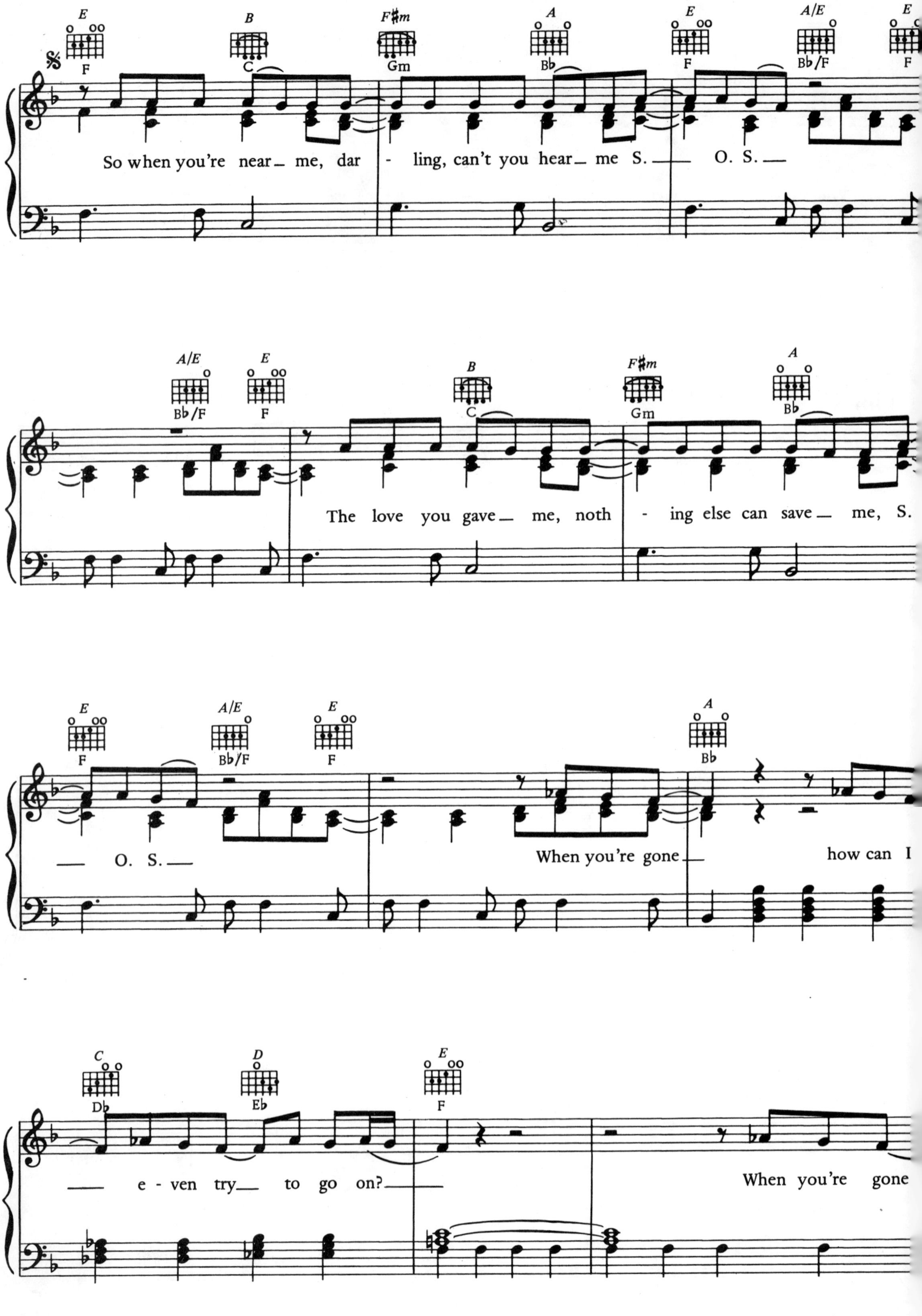

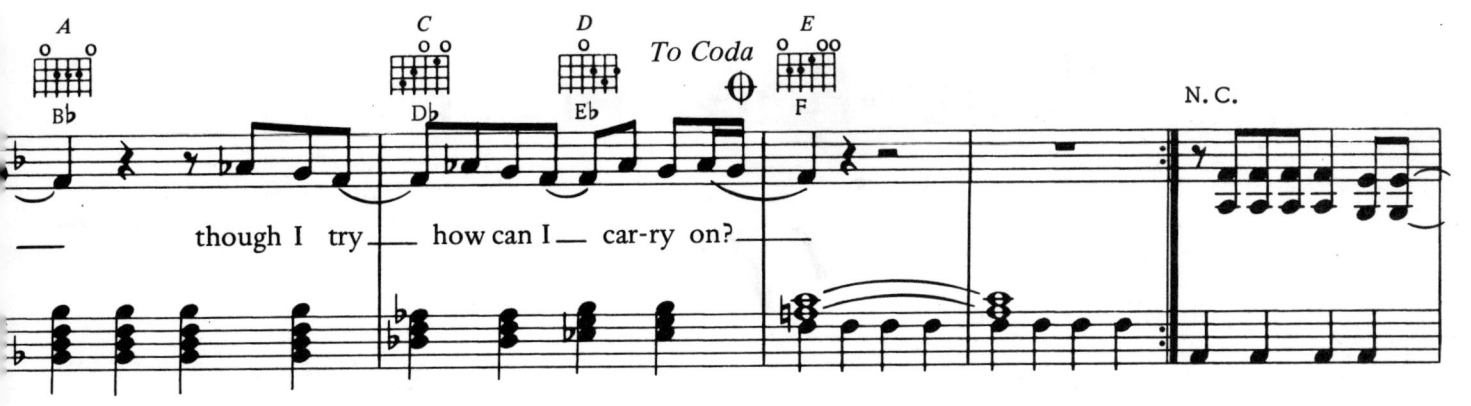

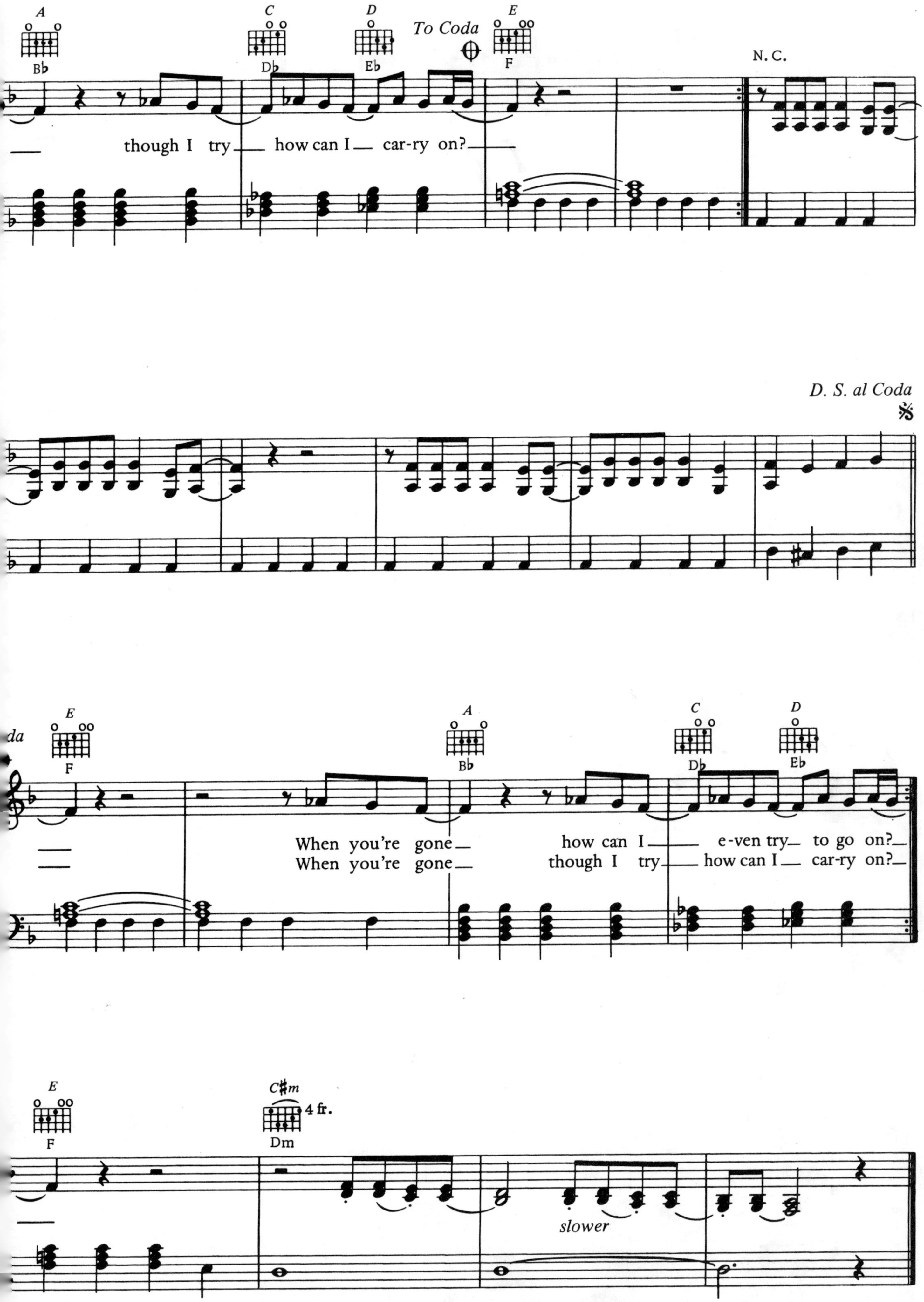

though I try__ how can I __ car-ry on?__

D. S. al Coda

When you're gone_____ how can I_____ e-ven try__ to go on?__
When you're gone_____ though I try__ how can I __ car-ry on?__

slower

245

Chorus

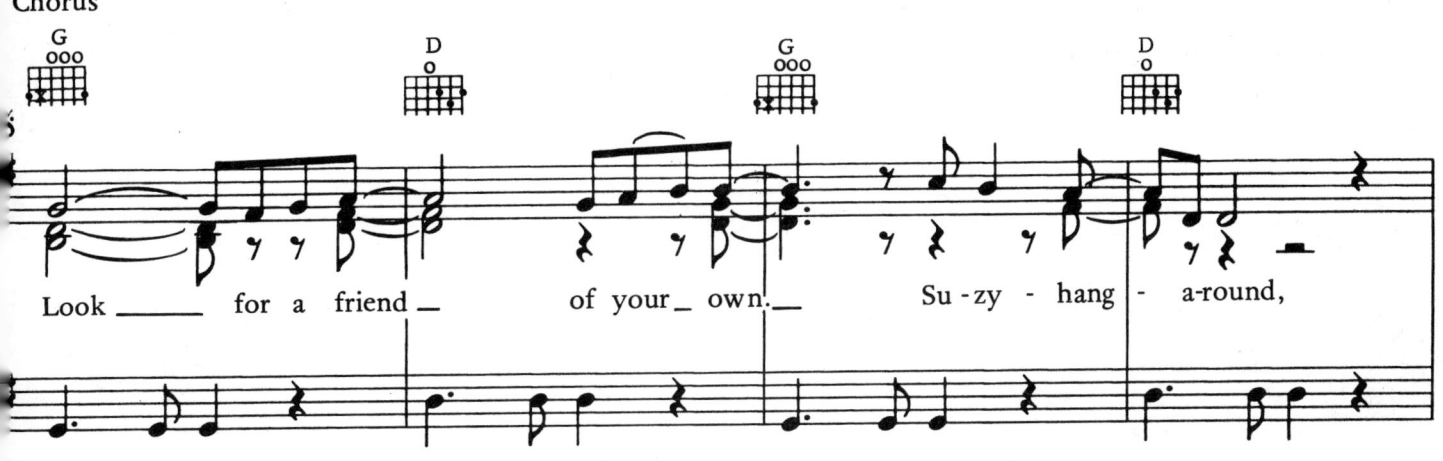

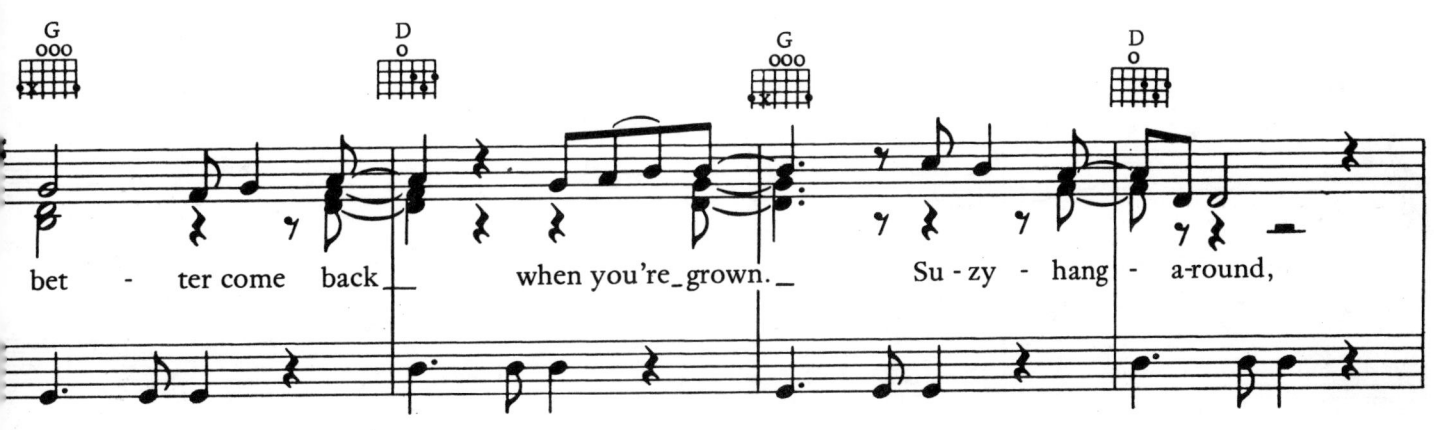

247

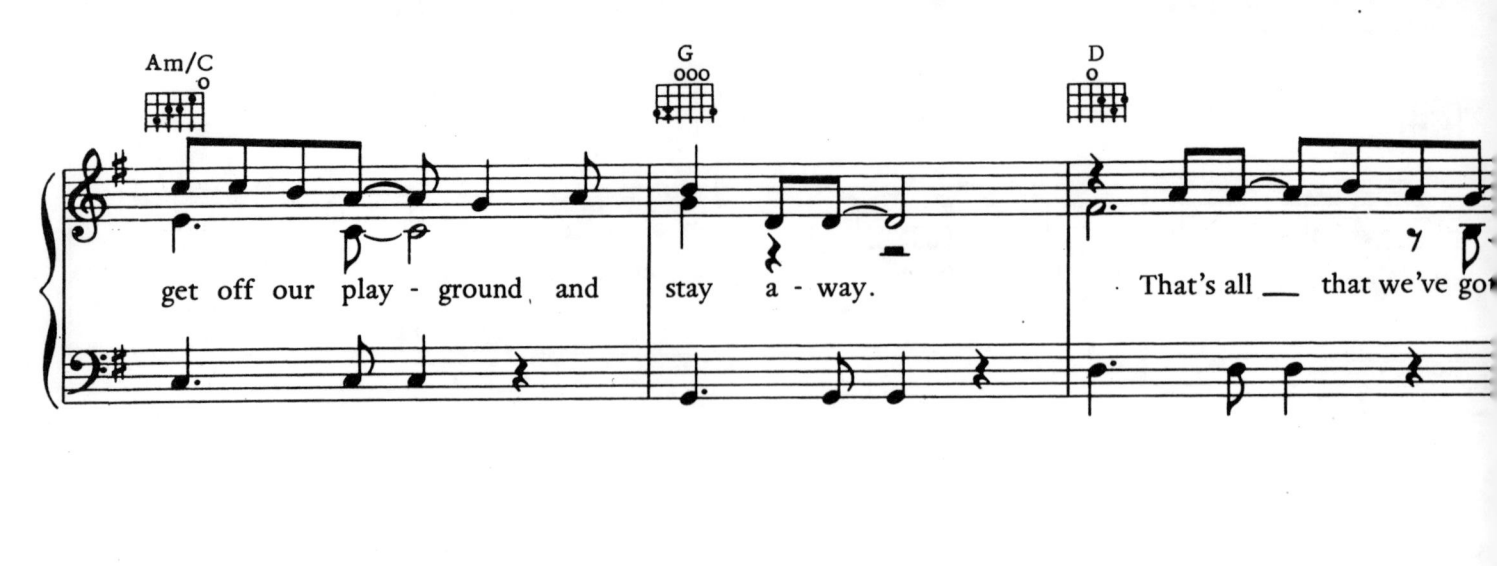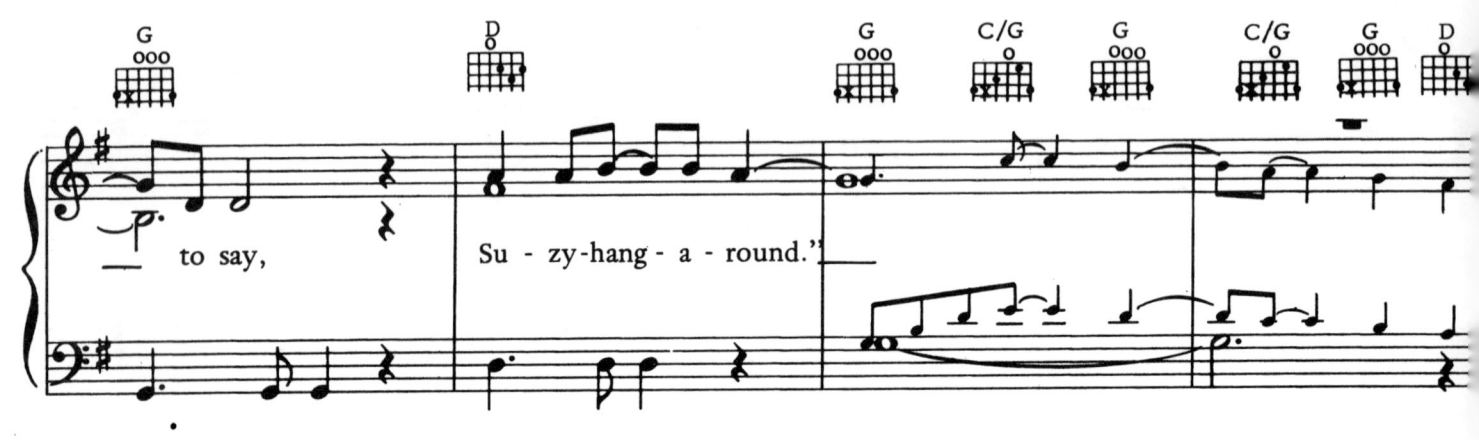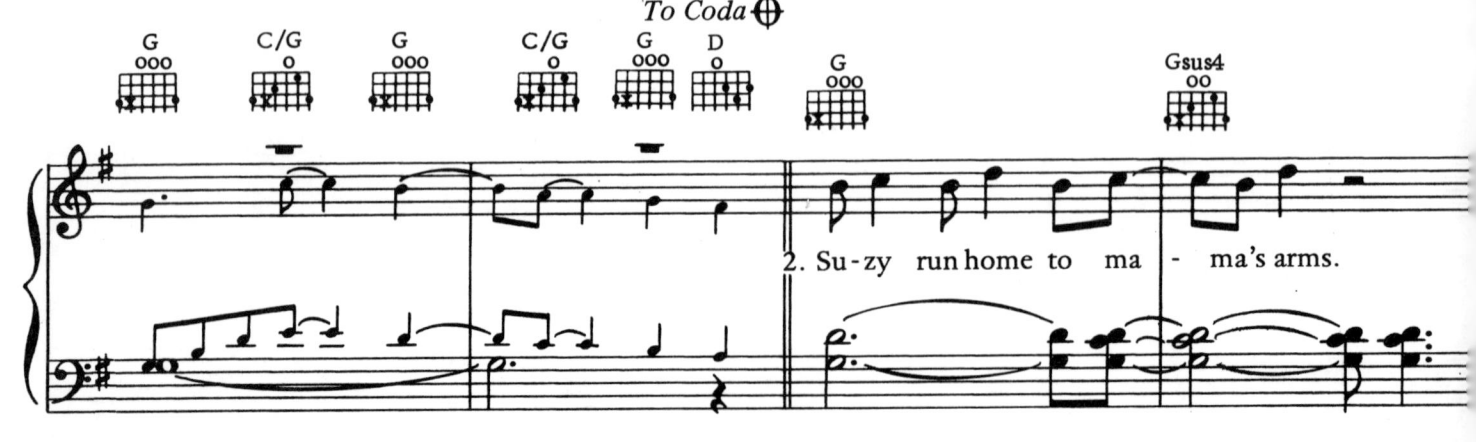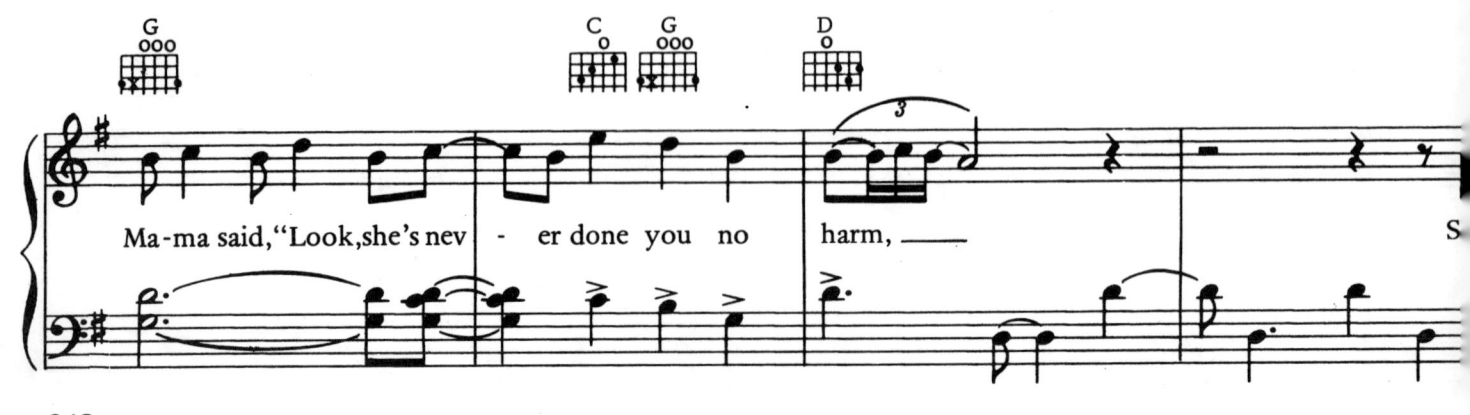

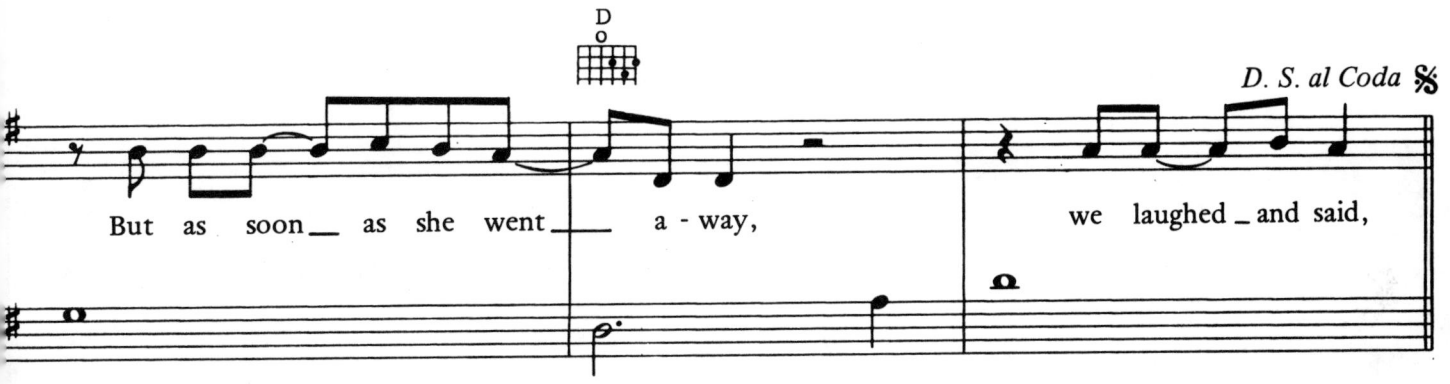
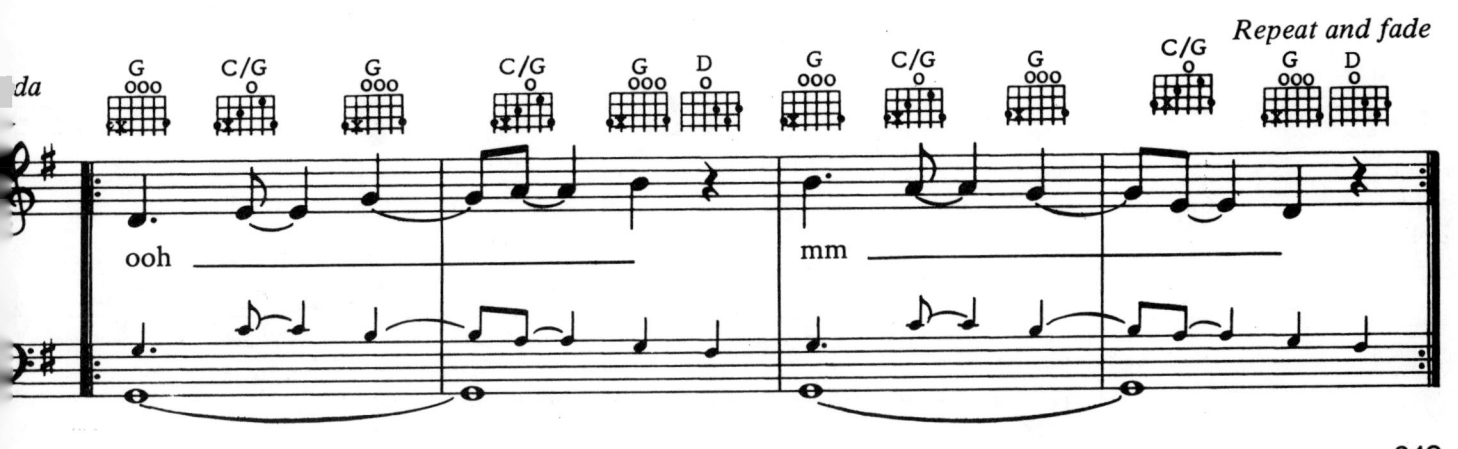

Take A Chance On Me

Words and Music by
Benny Andersson & Björn Ulvaeus

250

Copyright © 1977, 1978 Union Songs AB, Stockholm, Sweden for the world
Artwork Music Co., Inc. for U.S.A. and Canada
International Copyright Secured   All Rights Reserved

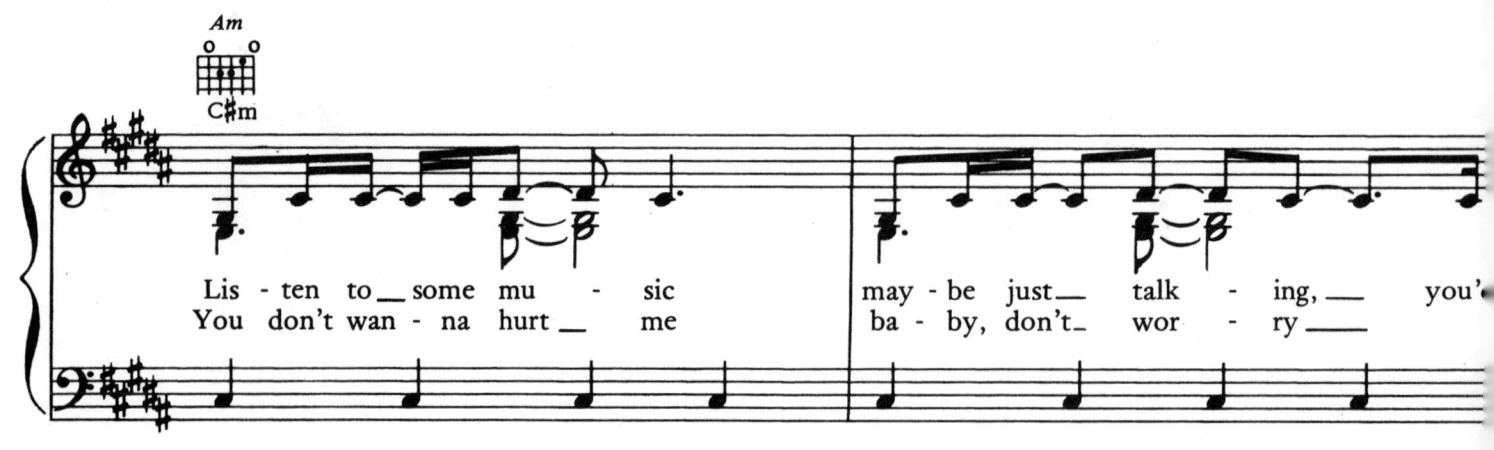

D
F♯
Gon-na do my ver - y best, ba-by, can't you see, got-ta put me to
G
B
Repeat and fade
the test take a chance on me.
If you change your mind

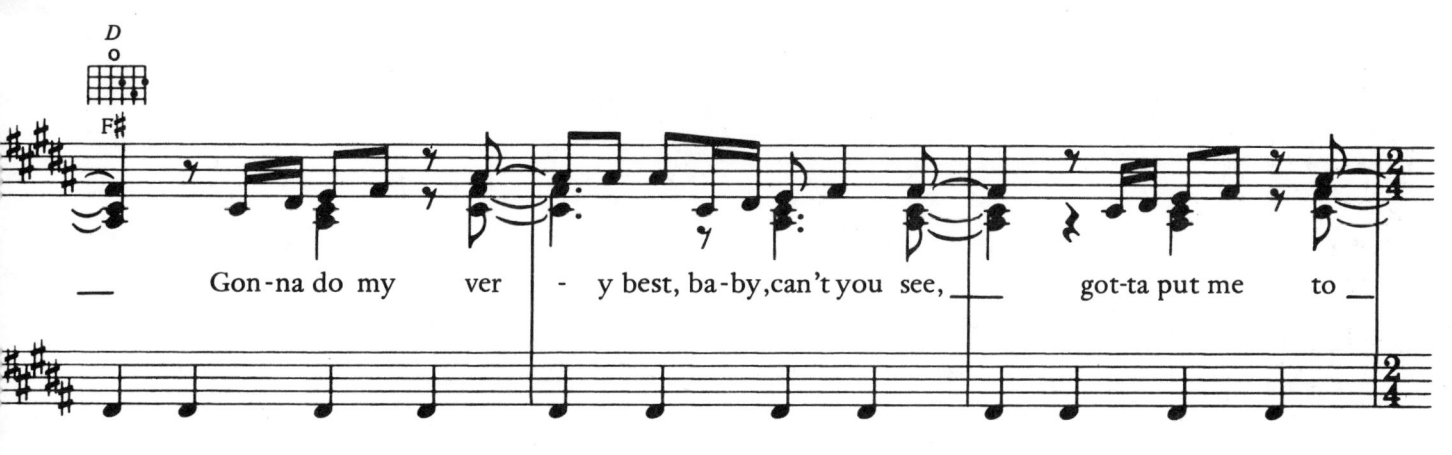

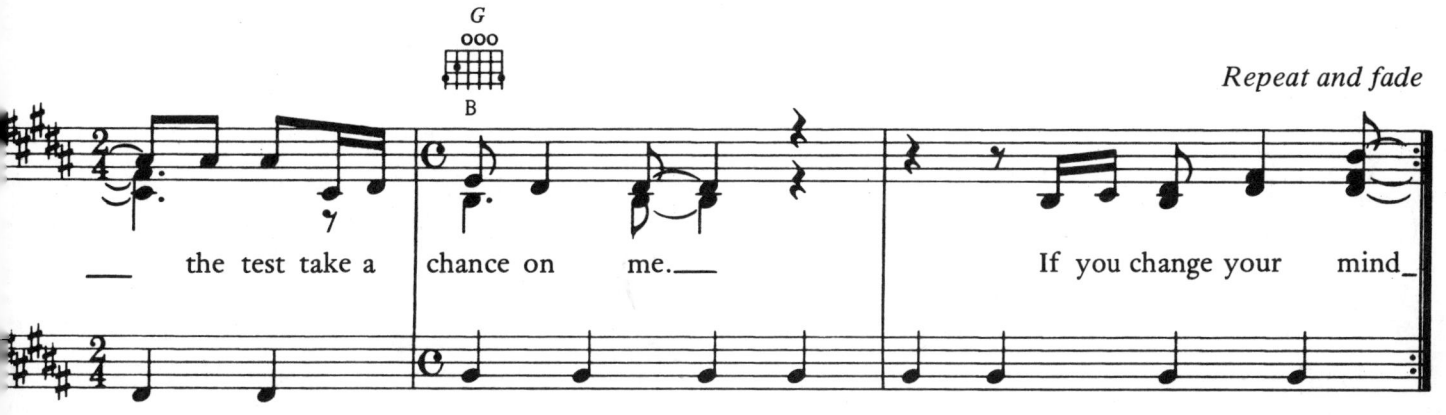

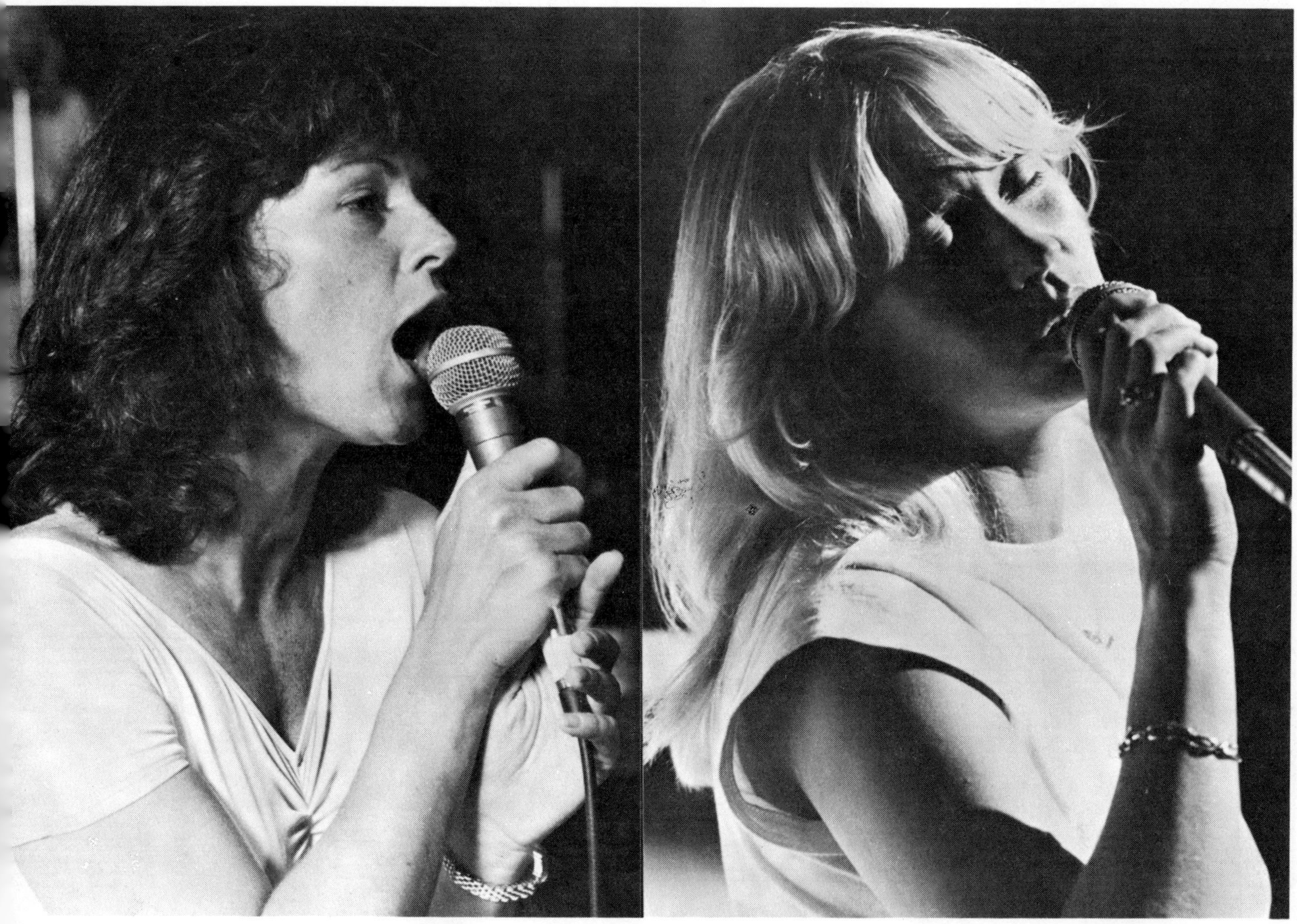

Tiger

Words and Music by
Benny Andersson & Björn Ulvaeus

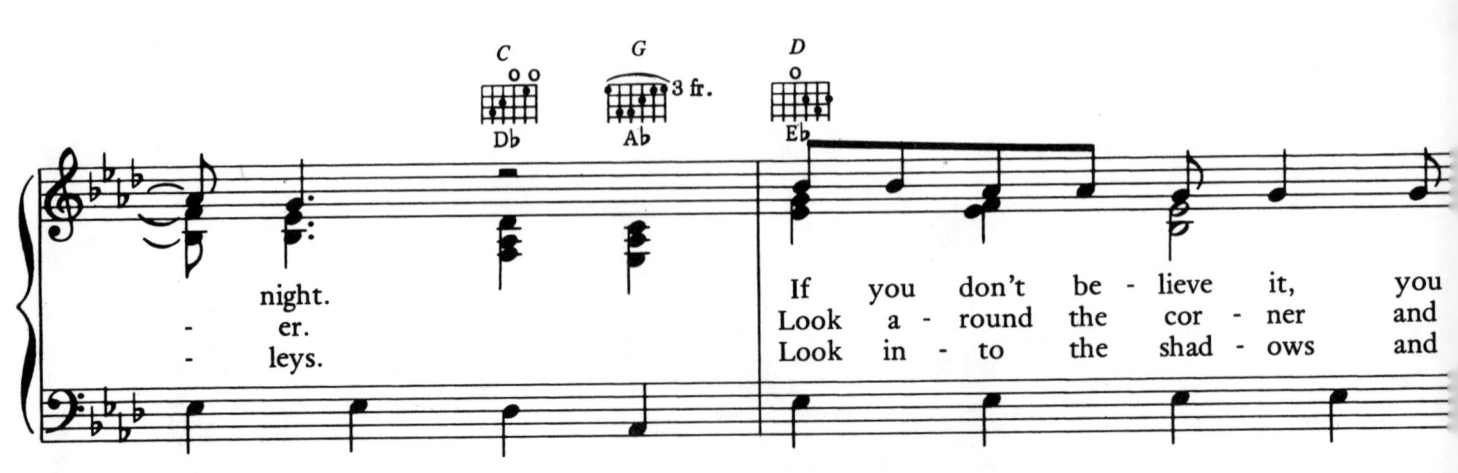

Copyright © 1976 Union Songs AB, Stockholm, Sweden for the world
Countless Songs Ltd. for U.S.A. and Canada
International Copyright Secured   All Rights Reserved

Tropical Loveland

Words and Music by
Benny Andersson, Björn Ulvaeus
and Stig Anderson

1. Come to my love-land, Wander a-
2. Come to my love-land, Wander with

long, Beau-ti-ful gar-dens full of
me. Lie with me, dar-ling, in the

Copyright © 1975 Union Songs AB, Stockholm, Sweden for the world
Countless Songs Ltd. for U.S.A. and Canada
International Copyright Secured   All Rights Reserved

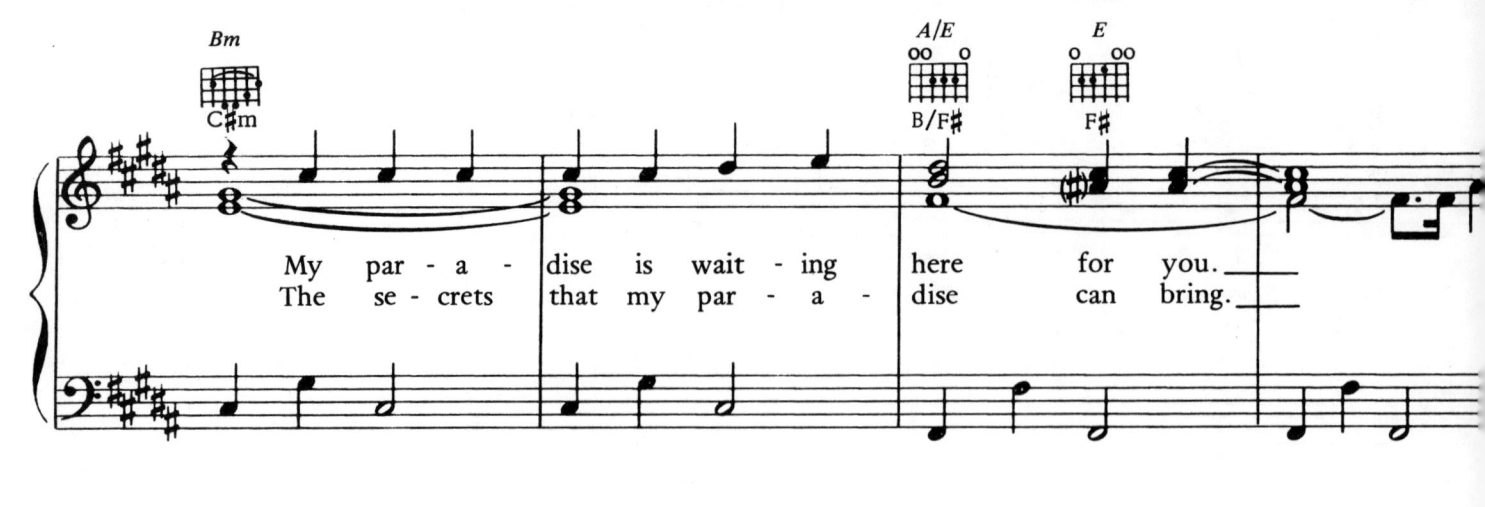

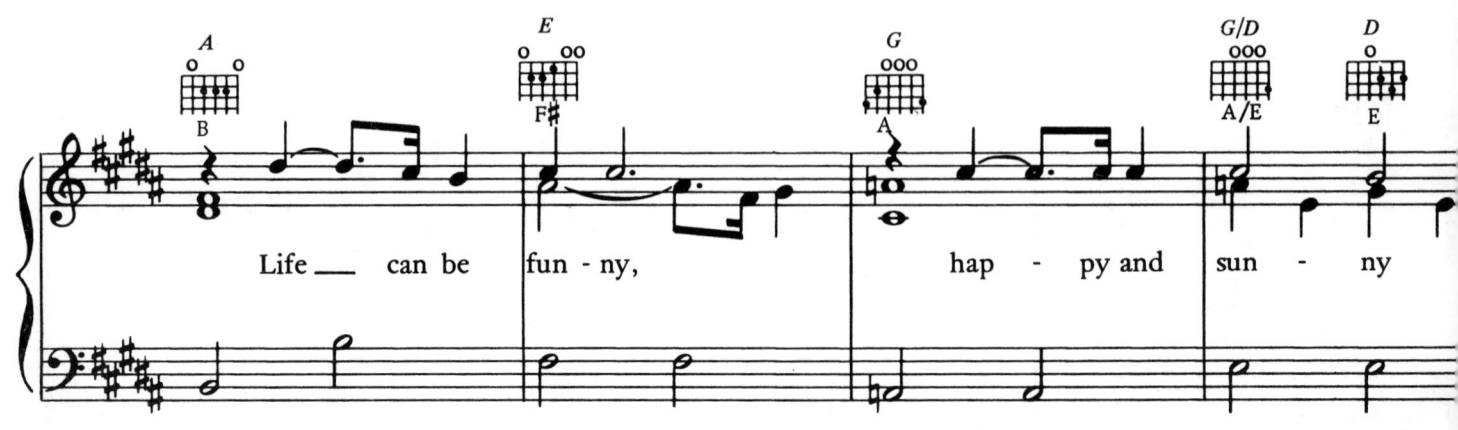

Watch Out

Words and Music by
Benny Andersson & Björn Ulvaeus

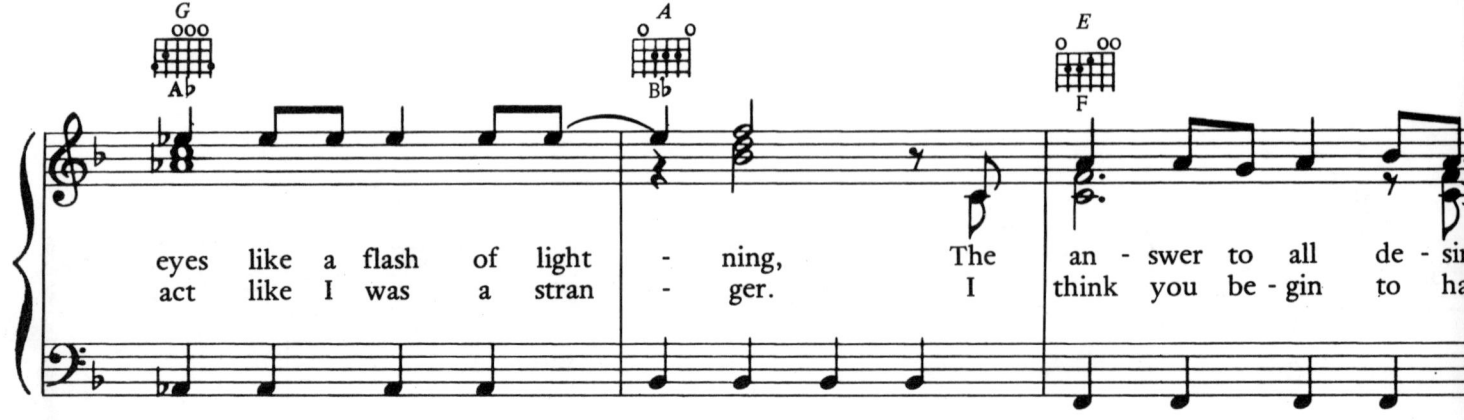

1. You move like a flame of fire, You eyes like a flash of light-ning, The an-swer to all de-sir...
2. It's been kind-a fun-ny late-ly, You act like I was a stran-ger. I think you be-gin to ha...

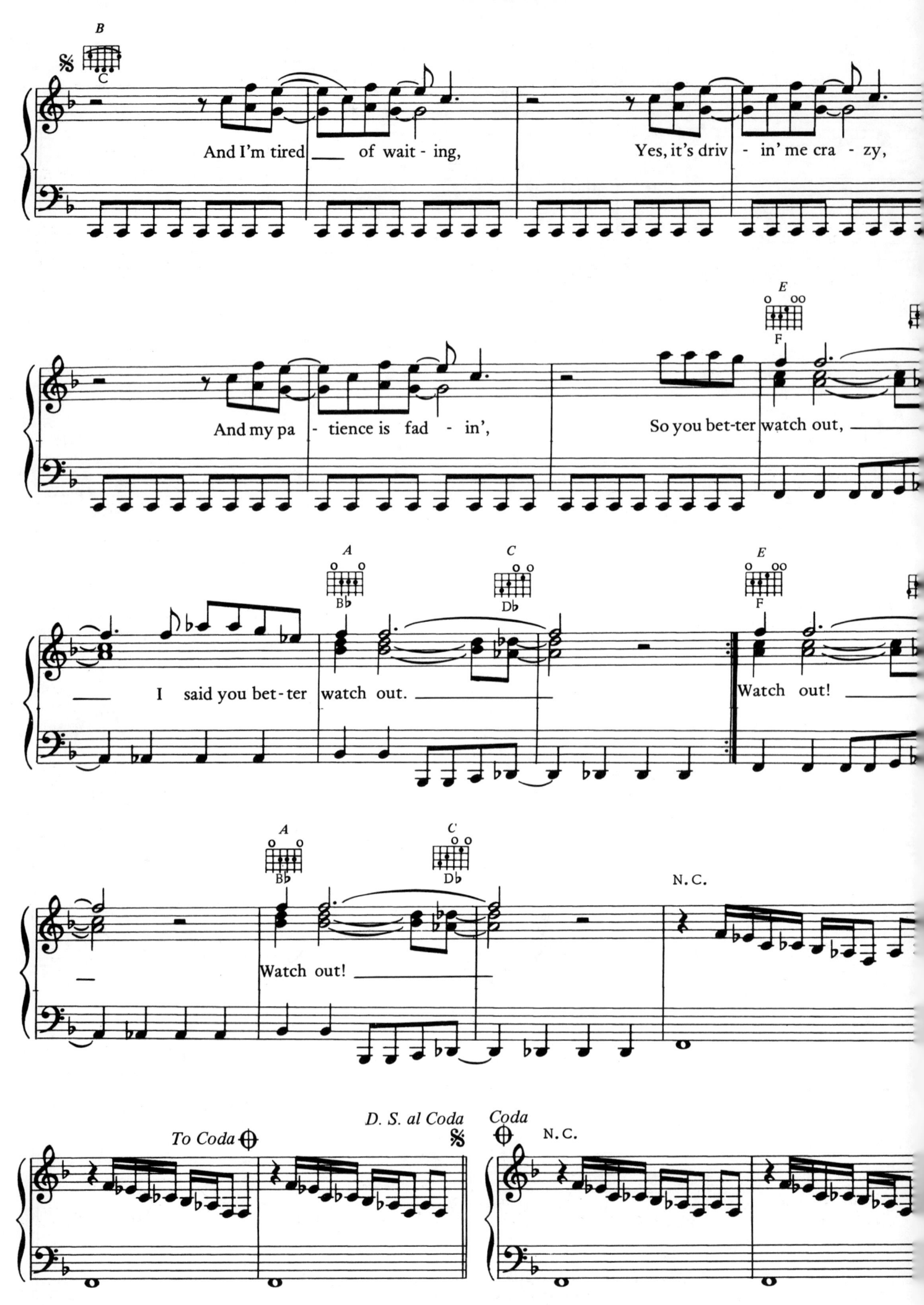

What About Livingstone

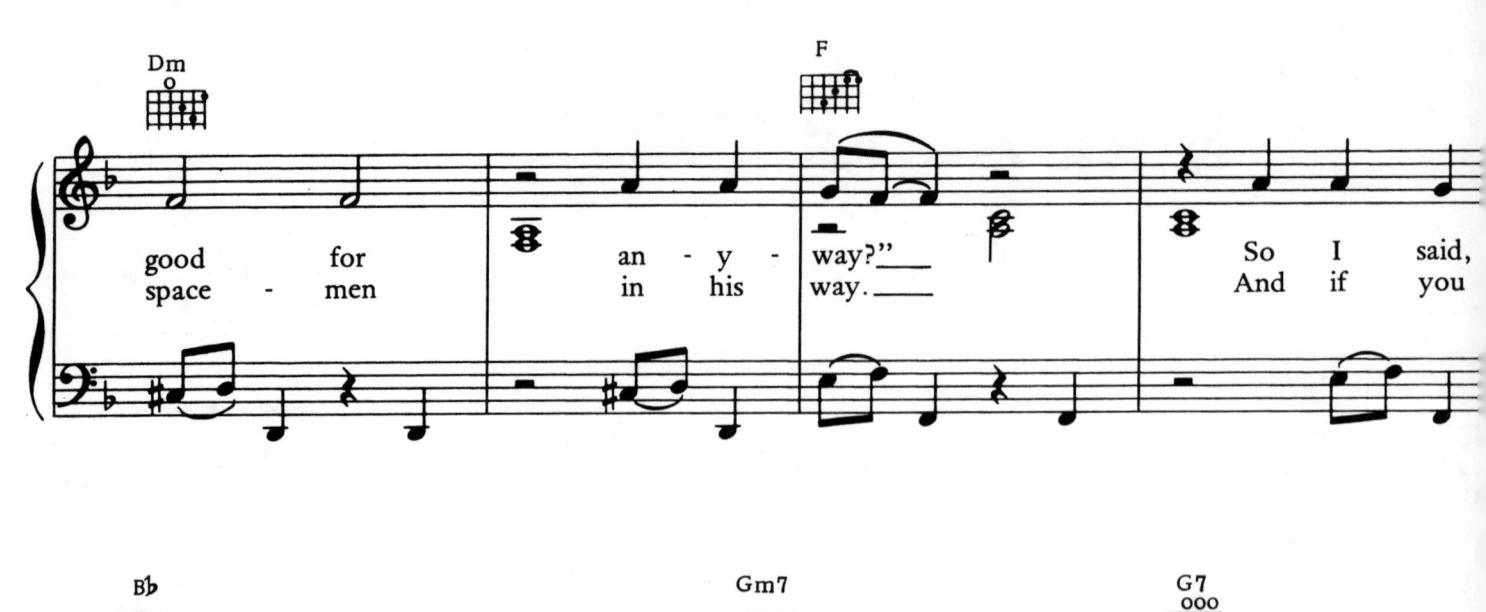

Waterloo

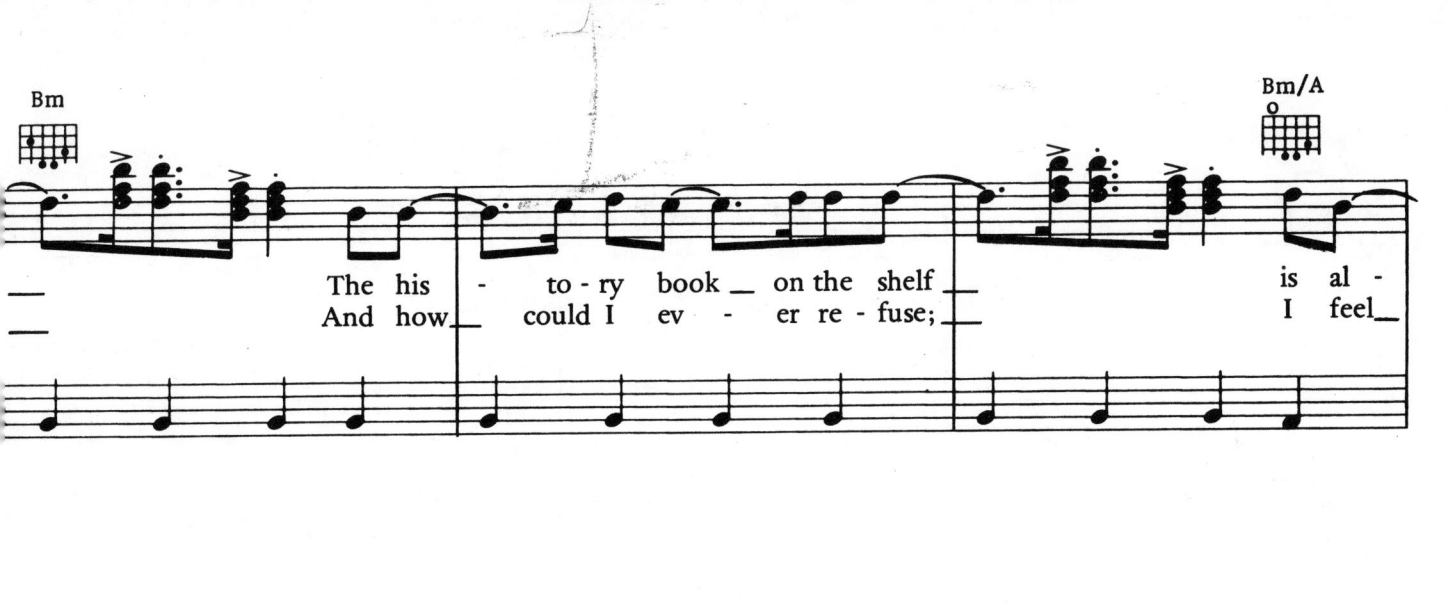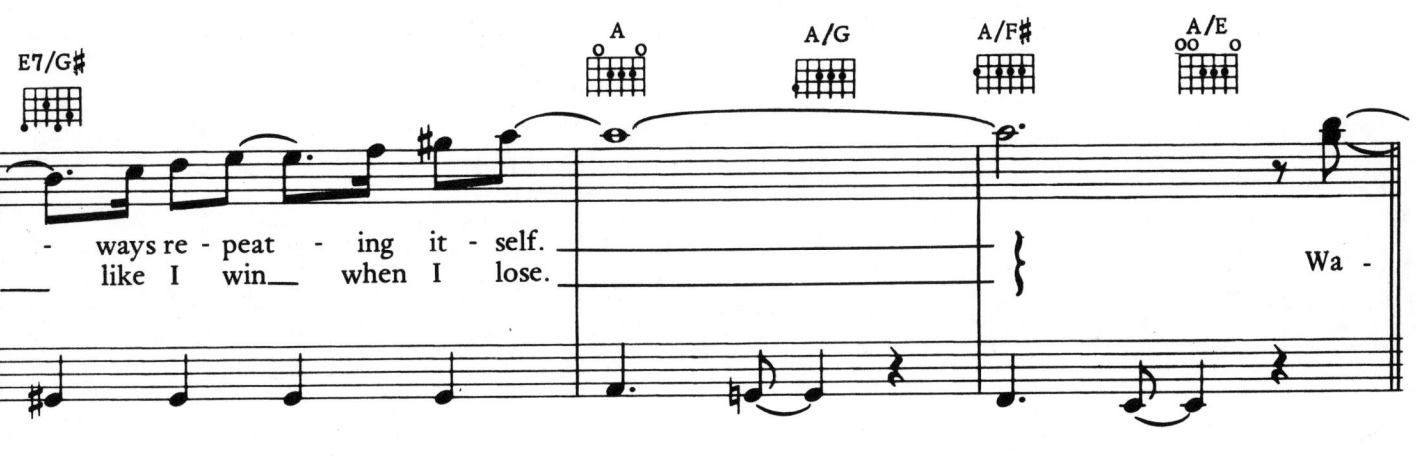

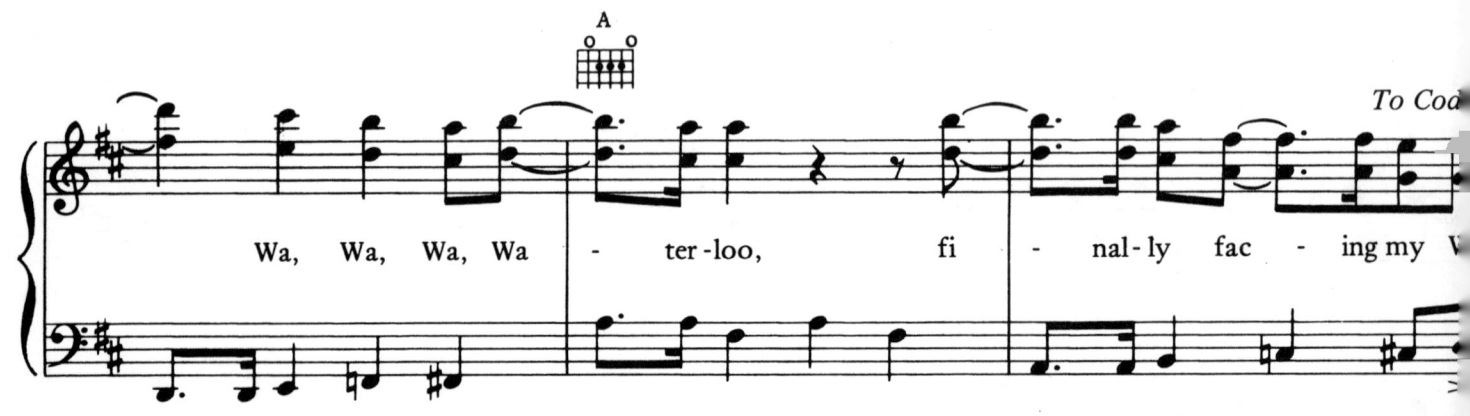
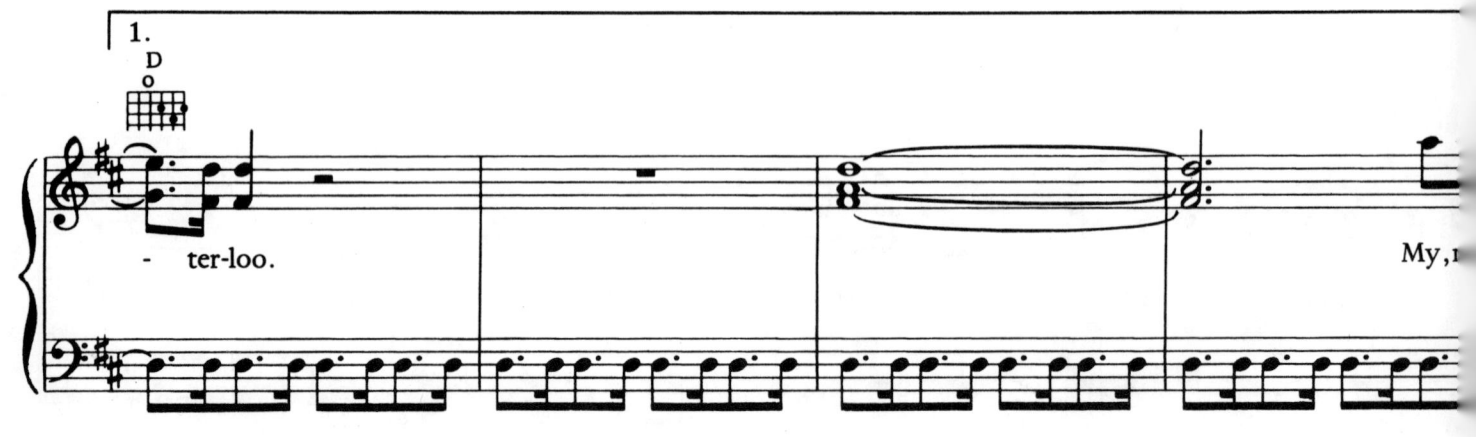

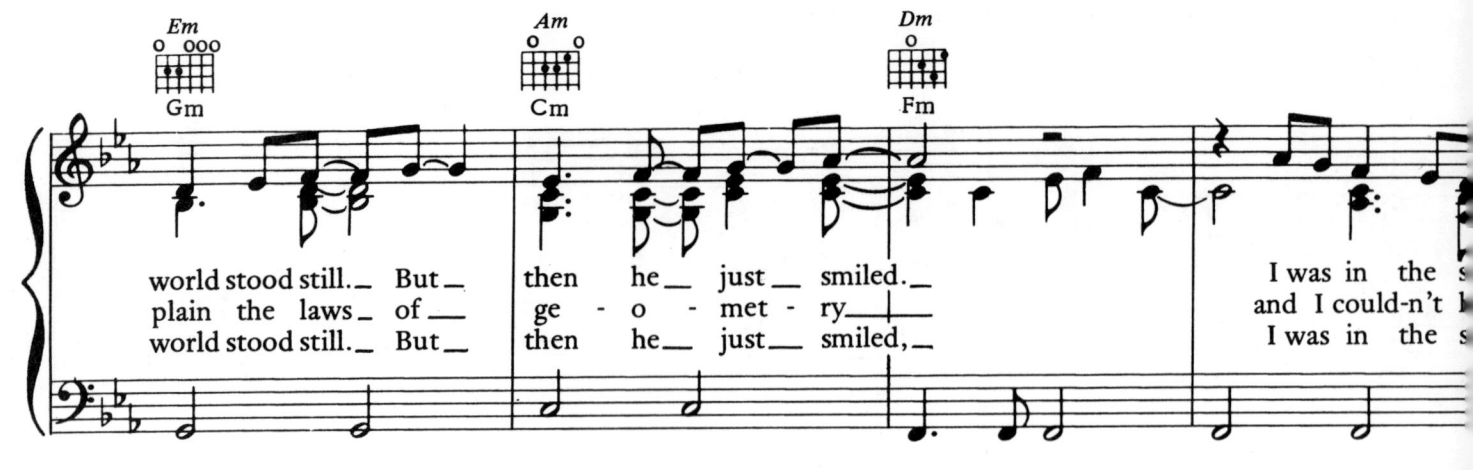

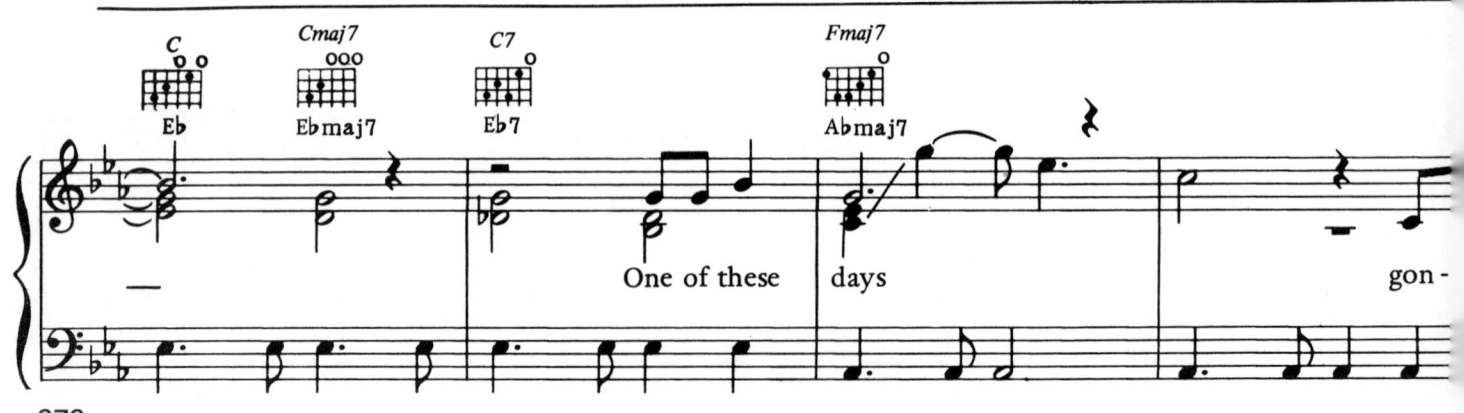

Why Did It Have To Be Me?

Words and Music by
Benny Andersson & Björn Ulvaeus

Boogie Rock

When you were lone - ly you need - ed a man,— some - one to lean— on, well I un - der - stand.— It's on - ly nat - 'ral, But why did it have— to be me? Nights can be emp - ty and nights can be cold,—

Copyright © 1976 Union Songs AB, Stockholm, Sweden for the world
Artwork Music Co., Inc. for U.S.A. and Canada
International Copyright Secured   All Rights Reserved

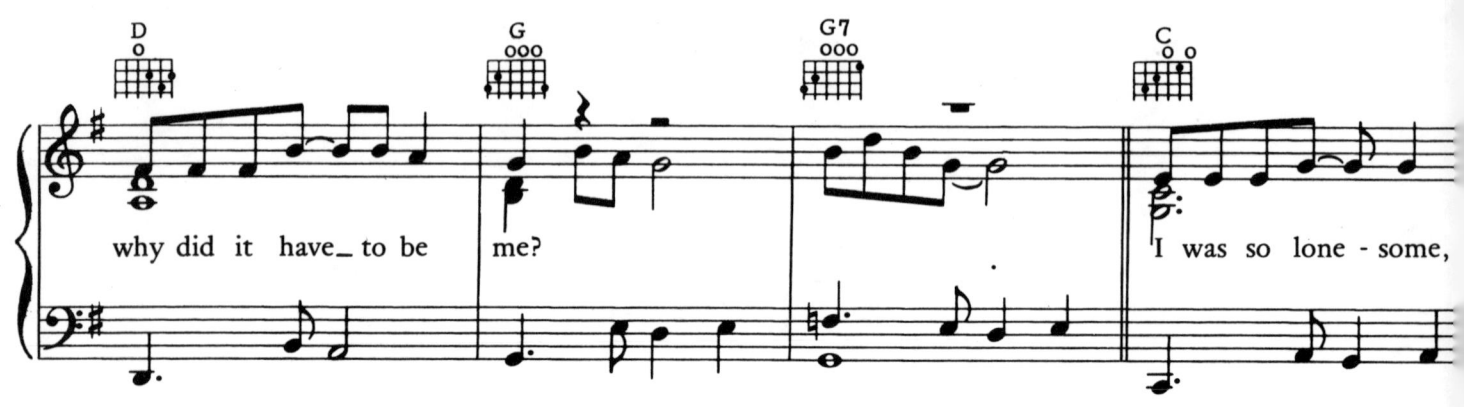

G7
C
3
I on-ly want-ed a
lit-tle love af - fair,
A7
now I can see you are
be-gin-ning to care.
But
G/B
ba - by, be -
C
lieve me, it's
A/C♯
5 fr.
bet - ter
G/D
to for - get me.
C
Gmaj7

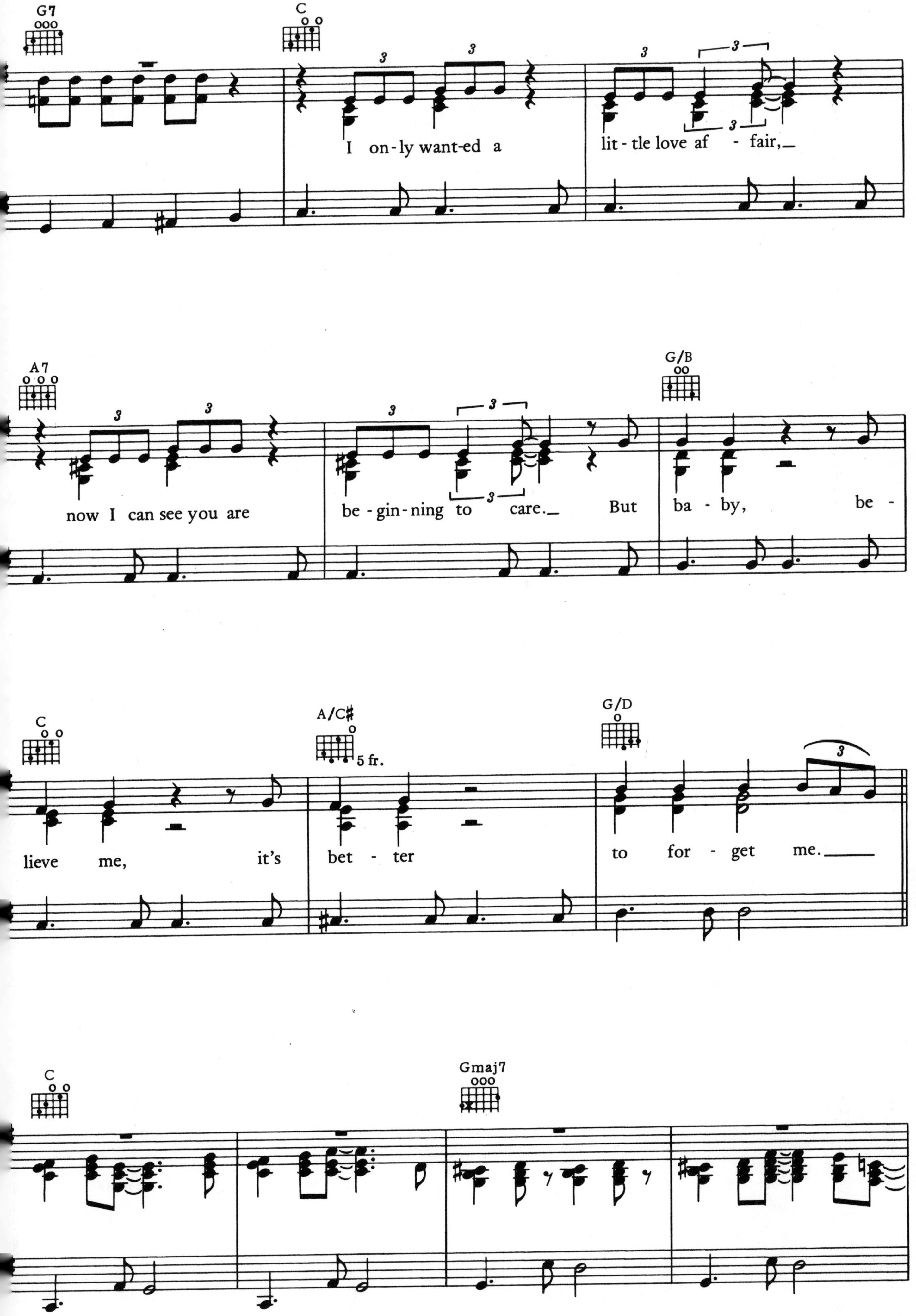

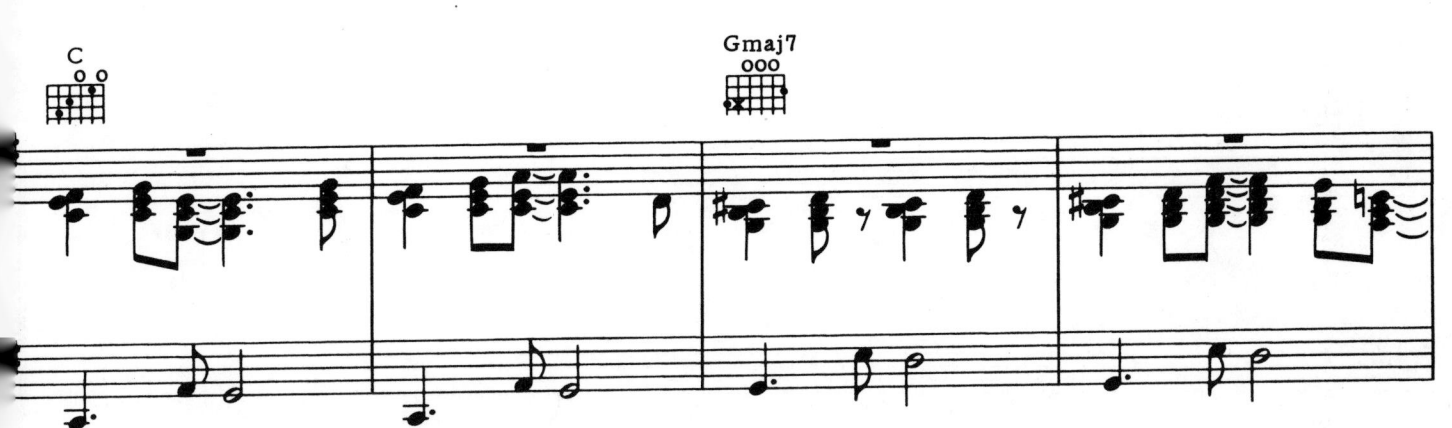

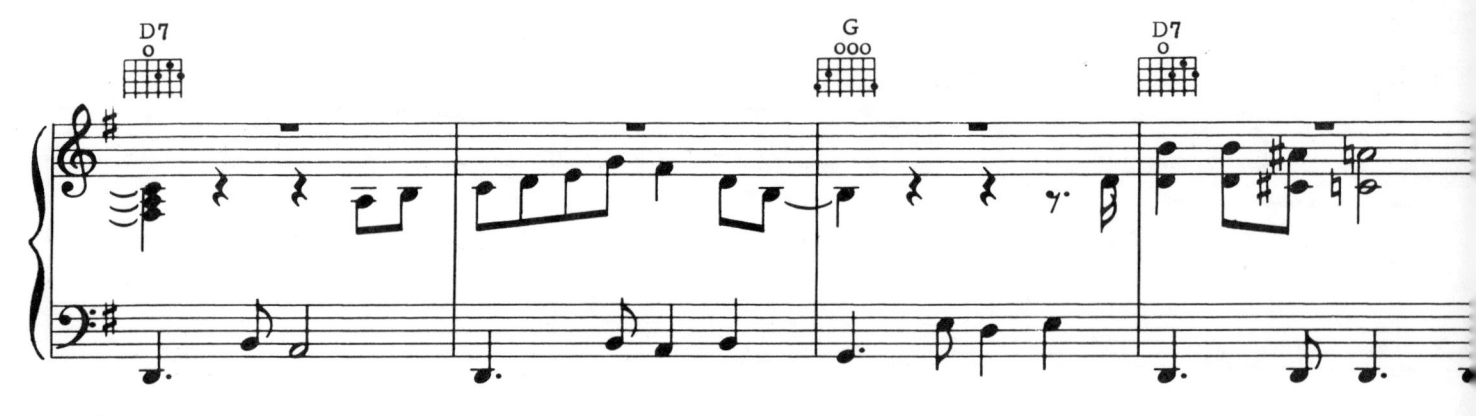

Photo: HANSER/POLAR MUSIC INT'L A

Songbooks
Edited by Milton Okun

THE NEW YORK TIMES
GREAT SONGS OF THE SEVENTIES This long anticipated songbook is a stunning musical documentation of the Seventies. Containing 81 of the best loved songs of the decade, it is expertly arranged for piano and voice with guitar symbols. Also contains photographs and an essay about the musical phenomenon of the Seventies. Includes AMERICAN PIE • BAD, BAD LEROY BROWN • BAND ON THE RUN • CRACKLIN' ROSIE • DANCING QUEEN • FEELINGS • I WRITE THE SONGS • JIVE TALKIN' • JUST THE WAY YOU ARE • LOVE SO RIGHT • LOVE STORY • MY LOVE • SEND IN THE CLOWNS • SWEET BABY JAMES • SUNSHINE ON MY SHOULDERS • SUPERSTAR • VINCENT • WE'VE ONLY JUST BEGUN • YOU SHOULD BE DANCING • plus 63 more.
Hardcover, Hidden Spiral $19.95
Soft Cover $9.95

THE NEW YORK TIMES
COUNTRY MUSIC'S GREATEST SONGS This superb collection of outstanding country favorites captures the spirit and style of country music at its best. Expertly arranged for piano and voice with guitar symbols, this handsome book features over 90 songs in 288 pages, a timely essay by Milton Okun on country music and photographs of America's best loved country artists. Includes BACK HOME AGAIN • A BOY NAMED SUE • DETROIT CITY • EVERYTHING IS BEAUTIFUL • GENTLE ON MY MIND • GREEN, GREEN GRASS OF HOME • HEARTBREAK HOTEL • JOLENE • KING OF THE ROAD • LITTLE GREEN APPLES • LOVE OR SOMETHING LIKE IT • MAKE THE WORLD GO AWAY • ODE TO BILLY JOE • OKIE FROM MUSKOGEE • PAPER ROSES • RUBY, DON'T TAKE YOUR LOVE TO TOWN • TAKE ME HOME, COUNTRY ROADS • TORN BETWEEN TWO LOVERS • WATERLOO • WOLVERTON MOUNTAIN • plus many more.
Hardcover, Hidden Spiral $16.95
Soft Cover $9.95

THE NEW YORK TIMES
GREAT SONGS OF THE SIXTIES ALFIE • BLOWIN' IN THE WIND • ODE TO BILLY JOE • BRIDGE OVER TROUBLED WATER • HEY JUDE • DOWNTOWN • GENTLE ON MY MIND • THE IMPOSSIBLE DREAM • RAINDROPS KEEP FALLIN' ON MY HEAD • A TIME FOR US (Love Theme from "Romeo and Juliet") • WE SHALL OVERCOME • YESTERDAY...82 great songs in all. Arranged for piano and voice with guitar chord diagrams.
Hard Cover, Hidden Spiral $17.50
Soft Cover $8.95

THE NEW YORK TIMES
GREAT SONGS OF THE SIXTIES, VOLUME 2 CLOSE TO YOU • FIRE AND RAIN • HERE COMES THE SUN • HOLLY HOLY • MICHELLE • MR. BOJANGLES • MY SWEET LADY • PUFF THE MAGIC DRAGON • WITH A LITTLE HELP FROM MY FRIENDS • FOLLOW ME • ME AND BOBBY McGEE • GUANTANAMERA • THE MARVELOUS TOY • THE NIGHT THEY DROVE OLD DIXIE DOWN • THESE BOOTS ARE MADE FOR WALKING • YELLOW SUBMARINE. 64 great songs in all. Arranged for piano and voice with chord diagrams for guitar.
Hard Cover, Hidden Spiral $14.95
Soft Cover $7.95

THE NEW YORK TIMES
GREAT SONGS OF LENNON & McCARTNEY YESTERDAY • MICHELLE • SGT. PEPPER • PLEASE PLEASE ME • HELP • WITH A LITTLE HELP FROM MY FRIENDS and 67 more great titles in fresh arrangements that capture the original Beatles sound.
Hard Cover, Hidden Spiral $17.50
Soft Cover $9.95

THE KENNY ROGERS SONGBOOK This definitive collection contains 23 of Kenny's most memorable tunes arranged for piano and voice with guitar chord diagrams. The songs include his earlier favorites such as JUST DROPPED IN • LUCILLE • RUBY, DON'T TAKE YOUR LOVE TO TOWN as well as many current hits; SHE BELIEVES IN ME • THE GAMBLER and COWARD OF THE COUNTY. The folio also features full color and black and white photos, discography, performance suggestions, and biography.
$7.95

THE SONGS OF BOB DYLAN FROM 1966 THROUGH 1975 A decade of Bob Dylan's songs have been collected in this handsome book. The 121 songs include: JUST LIKE A WOMAN • I'LL BE YOUR BABY TONIGHT • LAY, LADY, LAY • KNOCKIN' ON HEAVEN'S DOOR • FOREVER YOUNG • I SHALL BE RELEASED and HURRICANE. The songs have been expertly arranged by Ronnie Ball and Milton Okun for piano, voice and guitar.
Hard Cover, Hidden Spiral $19.95
Soft Cover $9.95

AN EVENING WITH JOHN DENVER All 23 songs from this great double album including ANNIE'S SONG • GRANDMA'S FEATHER BED • MY SWEET LADY • ROCKY MOUNTAIN HIGH • SWEET SURRENDER • THANK GOD I'M A COUNTRY BOY plus 12 pages of color photos.
$7.95

Obtainable at your local music dealer or by sending check or money order to:
WINTER HILL MUSIC Ltd. /P.O. Box 4247 • GREENWICH, CONNECTICUT 06830
(Please add 50¢ postage and handling plus sales tax where applicable). Free catalogue available upon request.